Connecticut Cryptids

A field guide to the weird and wonderful
creatures of the Nutmeg State

Written by
Patrick Scalisi

Illustrated by
Valerie Ruby-Omen

Pat

For Crystal: May our home always be a way station
for both cats and cryptids.

Val

To my twin sibling and co-conspirator, Finn:
May we always find a way to "Make CT Weird."

cryptid

noun

cryp·tid | \ ‘krip-təd \

plural: cryptids

An animal (such as Sasquatch or the Loch Ness Monster) that has been claimed to exist but never proven to exist.

- Merriam-Webster online dictionary

Contents

Introduction

Some years ago, I don't remember exactly when, Val and her spouse, Dee, began hosting art nights at their home for all kinds of local artistic types to gather and share their work. It was during one of these events that Val and I learned about our shared love of cryptozoology, me having obtained a certificate in cryptid field observation from Nutmeg State University and she having achieved a certificate in cryptid illustrative works from Constitution State College. We spoke longingly about the Mothman and the Fresno Nightcrawlers and, of course, about Connecticut's most famous cryptid, the Black Dog of the Hanging Hills.

It was during another of these art nights that I mentioned a creature I had just learned about (the Higganum Mucket) and bemoaned the fact that no one had written a comprehensive study of Connecticut cryptids.

"Why don't *we* do it?" Val asked.

I was so stunned as to be rendered momentarily speechless. In fact, it had never once occurred to me to undertake the daunting task of cataloging Connecticut's unique cryptids. But the more we discussed the matter, the more excited I became. And so, at the start of 2021, we began our grand expedition around the state to seek out and shed light on Connecticut's cryptid population.

It wasn't easy. For every hour spent pouring over old newspapers, we spent twice that amount of time in the rain, the cold, and the heat of our state's four seasons. At some turns, we were met with shocking hostility; at others, confusion. Val lost the smallest toe on her right foot to frostbite during one winter expedition, while I scarred my buttocks during a run-in with a nasty piece of rebar in the woods.

But when we found them — oh, it was wonderful! Sometimes it was just a glimpse; at other times we were able to watch for hours unfettered. I wrote my observations on note cards, while Val grew accustomed to sketching quickly — a must, since it is widely known that cryptids as a collective are adverse to all kinds of photography.

What follows is the sum of our research, presented as a field guide for seeking out and identifying these creatures on your own. Be warned, however, that this is not an undertaking to be done lightly. All readers of this book are hereby warned to search for Connecticut's cryptids AT THEIR OWN RISK and to hold blameless the creators of this book in case of accidental injury, maiming, burning, scarring, disfigurement, flogging, flaying, drowning, or death.

Proceed with caution.

Important Note

Each chapter includes a general history of the area
and creature in question, followed by descriptive field
observations and any sketches that Val was able to make.
You'll sometimes see additional notes or tidbits at the end
of some chapters. This book is arranged geographically by
region, moving roughly west to east.

SOUTHWESTERN CONNECTICUT

*Brookfield, Danbury, New Fairfield,
New Milford & Sherman*

The Candlewood Lake Monster

Among **Connecticut's** several ghost towns is the community known as Jerusalem in present-day New Milford. Unlike villages that were abandoned after industry dried up, the people of Jerusalem didn't leave voluntarily. Rather, they were forced out when Connecticut Light & Power (CL&P, now Eversource) finalized its plan to create Candlewood Lake. Between 1926 and 1928, the power company convinced people to move, cleared thousands of acres of forest and farmland, demolished buildings, built dams, and relocated more than 400 gravesites.

The work did not always go smoothly.

To implement its plan for a power generation reservoir, CL&P had to purchase properties from about 35 families in the proposed flood zone, which was known at that time as "Big Basin." Most owners sold willingly, but others did not. In the end, it didn't matter because CL&P claimed eminent domain. One book published a full 10 years after the fact still spoke about "the power company" with obvious disdain, refusing to call the utility by its proper name.

Today, Candlewood Lake is the largest body of water in the state and is bordered by five communities: Brookfield,

Danbury, New Fairfield, New Milford, and Sherman. The lake is a favorite recreation spot for both Connecticutians and New Yorkers, and its banks are home to some of the most expensive real estate in the area.

However, something besides the drowned remains of Jerusalem and Big Basin lurks beneath the lake's surface. Since at least the 1970s, stories have persisted about the so-called Candlewood Lake Monster.

Given that Candlewood Lake is manmade, it's reasonable to ask where this creature came from. Unlike Loch Ness or Lake Champlain, Candlewood Lake isn't a primordial environment disturbed by human intervention. Therefore, it seems unlikely that some kind of water creature was hibernating underground on dry land just waiting for the area to flood.

That being the case, CL&P becomes a credible suspect for the creation of the Candlewood Lake Monster. Notorious for its rate hikes, it's possible that the power company was up to something even *more* nefarious and made Candlewood Lake as a pretext for hiding an experiment that had grown out of the utility's control. Unfortunately, that doesn't explain the gap between when the lake was made in the late-1920s and when sightings began decades later.

We might also turn to the former town of Jerusalem for an explanation. CL&P's land grab obviously didn't sit well with some residents of Big Basin. Could it be that those holdouts whose property was claimed through eminent domain fed their malice into the very land itself, which over years and years incubated the creature we know today? If that's the case, then the Candlewood Lake Monster isn't a power company lab test gone wrong, but rather a supernatural agent of revenge for those whose land was taken a century ago.

Observations

Affectionately known as "Candy," the Candlewood Lake Monster's primary territory comprises the shallows around Vaughn's Neck. This peninsula juts into the northern end of the lake and separates the New Milford and Brookfield sides from the Sherman and New Fairfield sides. According to regular lake-goers, there are several prime picnic spots in the area, but few people dare to use them. That's because Candy is fond of bumping and even capsizing boats that wander into her domain, forcing the occupants to flee or risk being eaten.

While Candy's exact size and dimensions are not known, she is at least large enough to threaten boats up to 26-feet long, which is the general size restriction set by the Candlewood Lake Authority. In appearance, Candy resembles a giant walleye or bluegill, with a sleek body, protruding dorsal fins, and a powerful jaw. Since visibility is so poor for divers in Candlewood Lake, the creature's true coloring has never been observed.

Important Note

For more information about the area known as Big Basin that was flooded to create Candlewood Lake, see the chapter on Perry Boney on page 21.

Greenwich

The Grench

It is a common misconception that all cryptids are malignant by nature, or at the very least so far outside of human comprehension that their intent cannot be interpreted by man. However, this is not always true. Some cryptids simply want to teach people about municipal government. Such was the case in 1973, when the Greenwich Grench first came to wide public notice. It is important to note, though, that the creature is actually much, much older.

The true origins of the Grench are lost to history, but he has lived on the islands off the coast of Greenwich since before 1640. In the summer of that year, Robert and Elizabeth Feake bought most of the land that is today called "Old Greenwich." This included Greenwich Point, also known as Elizabeth's Neck, and several islands. Fearing discovery by the newly arrived Europeans, the Grench fled to Great Captain's Island to resume his solitude.

Part of the Grench's longevity is undoubtedly due to his long hibernation cycles. Not much is known about this process, except that one interval lasts 111 years. Thus, the Grench did not awaken for the first time on Great Captain's Island until 1751. It is said that he went ashore briefly to

see how things were developing in the so-called "Town of Greenwich" and that he talked to several people, including children. (It is not clear if these individuals ever spoke about the encounter.)

The Grench then woke in 1862 to find that the town's population had swelled to about 6,600. While eavesdropping at the mansions along Putnam Avenue, the Grench heard about the ongoing American Civil War and decided it was prudent to resume his hibernation. Unfortunately, the Grench's sleep was interrupted by the construction of a lighthouse on Great Captain's Island just five years later. Since the basement of the building had already been completed, the Grench snuck inside and was able to find a dry, quiet corner in which to continue his nap.

Then came the summer of 1973. Awakening once more, the Grench surveyed the completed lighthouse and observed the animals that were living on and near the island. He also saw the Independence Day fireworks that were being launched from the mainland. Regrettably, the July 4th holiday also brought visitors to the island, which was now accessible by regular ferry service. Dismayed that anyone could now come to Great Captain's Island whenever they pleased, the Grench set out toward Greenwich to learn more.

The Grench's experiences over the next year are chronicled in the Greenwich *Summary of the Annual Report for the Fiscal Year July 1973 to June 1974*. During this time, the Grench met most of the town's employees and learned all about how the Greenwich municipal government worked. Unfortunately, the Grench also discovered that he could not claim to own Great Captain's Island because he did not possess a deed to the property nor paid taxes on it.

There is, though, a silver lining to the story. At the September 1973 meeting of the Greenwich Representative

Town Meeting (RTM), the Grench was unanimously voted an *ex officio* member of all boards and commissions, and an honorary member of the RTM.

From there, the creature went on to have several more adventures. The Grench befriended a 14-year-old boy named Jamie, became a selectman for the day, and was eventually named keeper of Great Captain's Island. The Annual Report concludes, "If you ever want Grench, you will probably find him sleeping beneath a tree on Great Captain's Island."

This means that the Grench is likely deep into his latest hibernation cycle, which will end in 2084. The report does note, though, that the Grench can sometimes be found in Greenwich, which means that his sleep is probably broken by brief periods of wakefulness. Plus, the Grench can't sleep all the time if he means to keep watch of his beloved island.

Observations

Thankfully, the Annual Report is replete with illustrations of the Grench. He is about four feet tall with a round, spotted body, and clumsy, overlarge feet. In fact, one of the Grench's defining traits is that he often trips over his feet when he is excited or upset. He also has a large, dark nose, pointed ears, and a pair of antennae on top of his head.

The Grench is at home on either land or sea, and is capable of both walking and swimming long distances. Rather than take a ferry, he is comfortable swimming back and forth between Great Captain's Island and the mainland. The Grench also enjoys lounging in the water, especially during the summer months.

Prior to 1973, the Grench valued solitude, and his personality could best be described as "abrasive." However, his experiences in Greenwich between 1973 and 1974 gave the Grench greater insight into his place in the community. While the Grench still greatly values the sleep time he needs for his 111-year hibernation cycle, he is now much more willing to chat with visitors or even venture into Greenwich from time to time.

The Grench's true age is unknown, along with his expected lifespan. He is obviously capable of human speech. The name "Grench" comes from a contraction of the word "Greenwich" and not from the Dr. Seuss character, the Grinch, whom the Grench predates by more than 300 years.

Fun Fact

Carole Gewirtz Yudain co-created the Grench with famed cartoonist Mort Walker for the Greenwich 1973-74 annual report, which Yudain also wrote and designed. Walker, the creator of Beetle Bailey, was living in Greenwich at the time and provided the creature's original design. The report went on to win a first-place award from the University of Connecticut Institute of Public Service, which at the time offered training and professional development to municipal employees like town clerks and assessors. Helen Bridge of the Greenwich Finance Department even made a plush replica of the Grench that appeared in the *Greenwich Time* newspaper.

Of her experience working with Mort Walker, Yudain said that she would doodle different versions of the Grench's body parts, such as his legs or face. Then she and Walker would pick their favorite version, and Walker would do the final drawing.

The Grench

Cryptid Category: Semi-Aquatic

Notes: I had a wonderful call with Carole Gewirtz Yudain, who created the Grench with Mort Walker (deceased 2018). She was delighted that some people still knew about the Grench.

Bridgeport, Darien, Norwalk, Stratford & Westport

Sea Serpents

For as long as humans have looked out across vast expanses of water, there have been stories of unusual creatures lurking in the depths. Connecticut, with its long coastline and extensive maritime history, is no exception. Tales of serpents, mermaids, octopi, and more have circulated up and down Long Island Sound since before Colonial times.

You can drop a pin anywhere on the Connecticut coast and find at least a handful of stories about strange sea happenings, but the area between Darien and Stratford seems to be particularly active. Cryptozoologists aren't sure why sea serpents are attracted to this part of the state — or what sometimes drives these creatures as far east as New Haven, Old Lyme, and beyond.

Much of this region's documented sea serpent lore begins in the late-nineteenth century, though there are certainly stories from much earlier. What's of particular note is that sightings were so frequent that shoreline newspapers like *The Norwalk Hour* and *The Westport Advertiser* ran yearly updates between May and September. The papers were also quick to note years in which there were no serpent sightings.

A full account of all sea serpent activity in the area could likely fill its own book. Instead, let's focus on several particular instances in which the creature (or creatures) was clearly sighted and described.

In September 1878, a steamboat travelling to Stratford from Huntington, N.Y., encountered a snakelike creature with a wide-open mouth and a body whose circumference was as big around as a large horse. As the creature undulated through the water, its bulk formed arcs under which could be driven a team of oxen.

In July 1892, a sailor was passing near Scott Cove in Darien when he came across a ferocious monster nearly 80 feet long with the head of a bull and the antlers of a stag. It had a single eye in the center of its forehead and could expel water from its nostrils at high pressure. Unlike other serpents, this one had a rigid body with a fin at the extreme end of its tail that it used to propel itself through the water.

Between 1896 and 1897, Connecticut's sea serpents sojourned farther east, where they were spotted by nearly 200 people at Lighthouse Point in New Haven and by three Hartford men at Black Point in East Lyme. Sightings then occurred at Compo Beach in Westport in 1901.

In 1902, an oysterman caught a juvenile sea serpent at Gregory Point in Norwalk. The small creature was black on top with red stripes running down its flanks.

Two years later, campers on Cockenoe Island off the coast of Westport were startled by a serpent with yard-long sea green whiskers and teeth like closed umbrellas. The camping party assumed that the serpent had come to the island to eat its fill of field mice. Those in the party who were armed slept with their guns for the rest of the night.

A sighting in 1913 recalled the encounter from 1892, when a fisherman from New Jersey saw a serpent off the

coast of Milford. The fisherman claimed that the creature was about 50 feet long and had the head of a musk ox. However, a sighting in 1934 professed that the serpent had the face of a camel.

And the list goes on. Generations of residents and visitors have seen serpents off the coast of Connecticut. Some sightings have been just that: far-off observations of the strange and unusual. Others were close encounters in which mariners had to put their lives on the line to scare off these denizens of the deep.

While there are countless unanswered questions about these sea creatures, there is perhaps only one that really matters: When and where will they show up next?

Observations

Given the variety of descriptions over the last 150 years, most cryptozoologists agree that there are multiple species of aquatic cryptids living off the coast of Connecticut. Most are large and bear at least some resemblance to snakes, though the similarities often end there.

In general, the sea serpents of Connecticut can be divided into two categories: those that dwell exclusively in the water and those at home both on land and sea. The former are among some of the largest water-dwelling cryptids in the state, reaching up to 100 feet long. For reference, that's about the length of three school buses parked end to end. These creatures have a variety of physical characteristics, from horns to water spouts. It is hypothesized that they spawn in coves or near peninsulas.

The second category encompasses creatures that are able to come ashore briefly, either to feed or rest. This includes the serpent spotted at Cockenoe Island and those seen frequently in places like Lighthouse Point in Stratford and Black Rock in Bridgeport. Though the creature at Cockenoe Island had large teeth and whiskers, these cryptids are generally smaller so as to be more mobile on land for hunting.

All Connecticut sea serpents are marked by their unpredictability. It is advised that they be approached cautiously or, better yet, viewed safely from a distance. Though these creatures feed primarily on sea life, birds, and coastal mammals, they will not hesitate to snack on humans.

New Fairfield & Sherman

Perry Boney

Just as not all cryptids are malignant at heart, some actively seek the company of humans. This is exactly what the fae creature known as Perry Boney did for several years around the turn of the twentieth century. Not only did Perry operate what was known as the "Smallest Store in the World," but he was also much admired by his neighbors for the deep relationship he cultivated with nature.

On Feb. 25, 1928, Connecticut Light & Power (CL&P) began pumping water into the site that would eventually become Candlewood Lake. Before the area was flooded, though, it was known as "Big Basin" and was described in one book as "one of the wildest and most romantic sections of Connecticut."

Stories abound about Big Basin. The giant Paul Bunyan supposedly cut trees there, and the area's barn dances, jamborees, and clambakes were legendary. Nestled between all of these boisterous, outsize tales are ones about quiet Perry Boney and his Smallest Store.

No one was quite sure where Perry came from; he was simply *there* one day, running his shop as if he had just

emerged from the fairy realm. What was more certain was that Perry wasn't like other people. Children were convinced that he spoke to the elves and fairies that lived near Greenwood Brook, and everyone knew that Perry could talk to animals, as he did whenever he went to Sherman to buy supplies for his store. Along the way, Perry would inevitably meet a tame raccoon well known to the town. On their walk together, Perry would speak to the creature "in a strange tongue" and would make "a funny little whistling sound as a woodchuck does when he's pleased about something." Sure enough, the raccoon would wait while Perry bought supplies and then dutifully follow him back to the Smallest Store.

On moonlit nights, Perry was said to play the flute outdoors, though some dismissed this as merely the sound of the wind moving through the trees. Perry also had a keen, penetrating gaze that could look right in and through a person. What Perry saw, he never mentioned.

If Perry himself was unusual, the Smallest Store was stranger still. The shop was only large enough to admit two children or one adult at a time and was adorned everywhere with musical bells. There was a bell at the gate, at the front door, and on the shelf where Perry kept his cash drawer. The gate was set in a small brushwood fence that protected the petunias and candytuft that Perry planted year after year.

Inside the shop to one side was a kettle filled with soil and portulaca flowers. Legend held that Perry's love had planted the flowers but had died before they had bloomed. It is said that Perry tended to this plant even more tenderly than he did to the landscaping outside, if such a thing was even possible. Each year, just before the flowers went to seed, Perry would spread cotton netting over the kettle to protect the plant and ensure that it would continue growing.

There were also the goods that Perry sold — though this held something of a mystery too. Perry carried something to entertain children (possibly candy), as well as two kinds of snuff for the Swedes who frequented the shop. Owing to his affection for animals, Perry reluctantly sold shotgun shells, though most hunters learned not to buy ammunition from the Smallest Store. That's because Perry's "special" shells generated a powerful recoil, and were so loud and smoky as to scare off any potential game.

What was truly strange about Perry's merchandise, though, was that it didn't seem to generate any income. Perry allegedly sold all of his goods at cost: whatever he paid for them is what the customer paid. That being the case, the people of Big Basin wondered how Perry supported himself. This question was never answered.

The Smallest Store in the World lasted until the 1920s, when word reached the area that CL&P was buying the land and Big Basin was to be flooded. The plan to create Candlewood Lake had been approved in July 1926 and was completed two years later. But before that happened, Perry Boney left the valley in much the same way that he had arrived.

One day, another Basin resident named Chuck Munson passed by the Smallest Store and was greeted only with silence. Munson was a local legend in his own right who once ran a way station called the Sherman Light House before quitting to become a log hauler. His wagon route took him past the Smallest Store twice daily. For three consecutive days, Munson drove past the shop without seeing Perry. Then, on the fourth day, Munson decided to investigate. Perry was nowhere to be found.

That night, Munson told his family that Perry had gone and that the Smallest Store had been abandoned. However, Munson also coveted something that Perry had left behind: a painting titled "Custer's Last Fight" that hung prominently in the shop and was much admired by all who visited. In the days after Perry's disappearance, Munson took the painting and sold it to a New Yorker. When pressed about having appropriated the artwork, Munson justified his actions by saying that Perry would no longer have any use for it. That's because Munson allegedly found Perry's body when Munson returned to the shop to take the painting. Perry, Munson said, had died next to the kettle with one of the portulaca flowers in his hand.

To this day, it's not clear if Munson — a known drunk — was telling the truth. No one else saw Perry's body; they just knew that he and his shop were no more. In the coming years, all trace of Perry Boney and the Smallest Store in the World would be wiped away as Candlewood Lake flooded Big Basin and gave rise to a legend all its own (see page 6).

Observations

There is strong evidence that Perry Boney was some kind of fae creature, but it's difficult to assign a more definitive label. He was clearly not one of the little folk that are discussed in later chapters since he was able to pass himself off as an adult human, but there were other peculiarities about his appearance. He was small and lean, with a wild shock of unkempt hair and bright brown eyes. Visitors to his store noted that his gaze was particularly arresting, as if he was searching for something.

The source of Perry's income is likewise a mystery, since the Smallest Store never seemed to turn a profit. Perry didn't live in wealth, but he clearly wasn't destitute either. It's possible that he produced money by other, supernatural means, such as drawing gold or gems from the fairy realm. This is merely conjecture, though, since there are no reports of how Perry paid for the goods that he bought at the Sherman general store.

To this day, there are those who believe that Perry is not dead, as Chuck Munson claimed, but is instead still lingering in the wilderness around Candlewood Lake. On certain moonlit nights, it's not uncommon to hear music from Perry's flute, though skeptics will say that this is simply the sound of the wind coming off the surrounding hills.

Important Note

It's possible to roughly date the story of Perry Boney as happening between 1896 and 1926 based on the copy of the painting that hung in the Smallest Store in the World. "Custer's Last Fight" was painted by Cassilly Adams in 1888 and sold to Adolphus Busch, co-founder of Anheuser-Busch, in 1892. Most stories about Perry Boney incorrectly note that the painting was a whiskey ad, but "Custer's Last Fight" was instead widely used as a Budweiser Beer advertising print starting in 1896. More than 150,000 copies of the print were distributed, making it one of the most reproduced lithographs of its time. The original painting from which the prints were made was destroyed in a fire in 1946.

Perry Boney

Cryptid Category: Fae (fairy)?

Notes: Perry Boney is difficult to categorize because there is so much we don't know. Was he able to change his appearance? Did he merely appear human?

Stratford

The Lordship Mermaids

For more than 200 years, the iconic Stratford Point Lighthouse has helped guide travelers to port at the mouth of the Housatonic River. First built in 1822, the lighthouse originally had eight oil-fired lamps that needed constant attention, especially in winter. The current tower and keeper's dwelling were built in 1881, and the site has been home to multiple keepers, their families, and their assistants.

Among this illustrious line was Capt. Theodore D. Judson, who served as keeper from 1880 to 1921 with help from his wife and two children. By most accounts, the Judsons were well-respected, and Theodore took seriously his stewardship of the lighthouse. His daughter, Agnes, became a subject of high regard in 1897 when she rescued two men from drowning. And when Theodore was threatened with reassignment in 1914, the community outcry was so great that the transfer was cancelled.

In popular books and movies, the life of a keeper is portrayed as a taxing profession that can lead to loneliness, depression, hallucinations, and even madness. This isn't far from the truth. On Aug. 10, 1905, an assistant keeper

at nearby Stratford Shoal Lighthouse between Bridgeport and Port Jefferson, N.Y., tried to kill his fellow assistant and destroy the lighthouse lamp. At Stratford Point, there are anecdotes about a February blizzard in which Theodore had to operate the clockwork fog bell continuously for 207 hours — or eight-and-a-half days — with only one brief stop. The bell ran for 150 minutes at a clip but took 20 minutes to wind.

Obviously, Theodore wasn't immune to the pressures of his job, but having his family with him probably helped. That's what makes the events of Aug. 15, 1904, so compelling: Not only did others back up the story, but Theodore also claimed to have evidence of what had happened.

It was Monday, and Theodore was busying himself around the lighthouse property when he heard singing coming from the direction of the sea. Then, as now, the lighthouse is located on the southern tip of an anvil-shaped peninsula that juts into Long Island Sound. Since it was Theodore's responsibility to monitor the waters around the point, he quickly set out to investigate.

In moments, Theodore found the source of the "angelic" voice, which he described as stranger than any he had ever heard. It wasn't coming from a fisherman or even a couple out enjoying the morning sea. No, it was coming from a mermaid.

Theodore was transfixed. As he watched from the bluff, the creature sat on the rocks, unconcernedly brushing her long, golden hair. Thinking, maybe, of stories about the infamous "Fejee Mermaid" that late Connecticut native P.T. Barnum had displayed in 1842 or of the $50,000 bounty that Barnum had once offered for the Lake Champlain Monster, Theodore quickly decided to try and catch the mermaid.

Intimately familiar with the point after having been stationed there for 24 years, Theodore circled around to the west and tiptoed to the water's edge. He crept from rock to rock, getting closer and closer to the mermaid's boudoir, when he began to have second thoughts. "No muse I ever heard so enchanted me," he later told newspapers. Still, the prize was too precious to resist. With a final bound, he snagged the mermaid around the waist.

Not unexpectedly, the mermaid was quite displeased by this situation. She screamed and began struggling, striking Theodore on the head with her hairbrush and knocking his cap into the water. As the lighthouse keeper began racing back to dry land, the mermaid pulled his hair and whipped her tail around to cut Theodore's chin. Despite these injuries, he was almost there ...

With an undulating wiggle, the mermaid propelled herself out of Theodore's arms and back into the water. Theodore was stunned. He had been so close to victory. And was it just his imagination, or had the mermaid *laughed* as she sped away toward Long Island Sound?

As Theodore went to retrieve his cap, he noticed something else in the water: the mermaid's hairbrush! It wasn't much of a consolation prize, but it was proof of what had happened. He decided to keep the brush on display at the lighthouse for anyone who doubted his story.

That was the last time that a mermaid would venture so close to Stratford Point, but certainly not the last time that Theodore would see the elusive sea maidens. In recounting the story of the original encounter in 1915, Theodore said that he saw the mermaids again and again, sometimes in groups of up to 12 or 15. "They're a grand sight," he stated. Theodore's wife, Kate, and his assistant, Will Petzolt, also corroborated the story.

Theodore was in his 70s when he finally retired in 1921. Even so, he bought a house near the lighthouse to keep watch on his former post and, perhaps, on the mermaids that lived in the Sound. He died in 1935 at the home of one of his daughters. Notably, a death notice that ran in *The New York Times* mentions the mermaid incident. It called Theodore a "raconteur of salty tales" and noted, "Friends, who would gather to listen to his stories, could never get him to retract the mermaid tale."

Observations

Capt. Judson's vivid memory of the events of 1904 provides an excellent description of the Lordship Mermaids. He said that the one he tried to capture appeared as a normal woman to her waist and that she had a tail about three feet long instead of legs. She was very petite, about 75 pounds, and had "gazelle eyes," fair skin, and long, golden hair. This last characteristic seems to be common among the Lordship Mermaids. In describing a school of the creatures, Theodore said that they all had yellow hair and flashing scales.

Based on their observed behavior, it's clear that the mermaids live in groups. Theodore said they were most likely to gather in the early morning or late afternoon, preferring rocky areas directly off the coast. He also noted that the maidens were sometimes attracted by the sound of the clockwork fog bell.

There is some discrepancy between the two accounts about the mermaids' vocal abilities. In the original article from 1904, Theodore claimed to have been enchanted by the creature's singing and noted that she screamed when he grabbed her. But in 1915, he said she made a hissing noise, though he added that she had a tongue and very white teeth.

Of the mermaid's hairbrush, Theodore supposedly kept it on view at the lighthouse for more than a decade, though its location today is unknown. He theorized that the mermaids got their combs and brushes from the staterooms of sunken ships.

After Theodore retired in 1921, his assistant Will Petzolt took over as chief keeper. Petzolt did not report any mermaid sightings, but it's important to note that passenger traffic in Long Island Sound diminished significantly during the Great Depression. With fewer opportunities to explore sunken vessels, it's possible the Lordship Mermaids moved temporarily to a busier part of the coastline. And with the Stratford Point Lighthouse automated in 1969 (albeit still occupied by a Coast Guard family), there are fewer people watching for the mermaids' return on a daily basis.

The Lordship Mermaids

Cryptid Category: Aquatic

Notes: The sea spray was particularly strong around Stratford Point today. Am still trying to track down current location of mermaid's hairbrush found by Theodore Judson.

THE
NORTHWEST HILLS

Barkhamsted, Granby, Hartland & Simsbury

The 'Killer Cat'

Mountain lion sightings are nothing new in Connecticut (see final chapter), but when they appear in the same area again and again, it becomes more difficult to write the occurrences off as a mass delusion. When the sightings happen over the course of three years and are coupled with the violent slaying of local animals, one must ask if something more sinister is at work. This is what happened in the towns of Barkhamsted, Granby, Harland, and Simsbury between 1957 and 1960 when a "killer cat" stalked the area and left these four communities on edge.

It was a rainy winter morning, the day after Christmas 1957, when Hugh A. McInyre spotted a sleek, black animal slinking north on Rt. 20 in Granby. The creature, she said, was about four feet and had a long tail. It strolled into the tall grass next to the road before disappearing from view.

McInyre called the police, who sent Chief Constable Harrison Hotchkiss to investigate. Hotchkiss, a former game hunter, could find no trace of the animal but suggested that McInyre might have seen a mountain lion, catamount, or puma. Of course, the Connecticut Board of Fisheries and Game, predecessor to the state Department of Energy and

Environmental Protection (DEEP), denied that such cats live in Connecticut.

Things were quiet until June 18, 1959, when a truck driver spotted a similar creature on Rt. 20. That same day, Granby Dog Warden Hans Groper was driving down Simsbury Road, about four miles away, when the creature pounced in front of Groper's car. The descriptions given by both men and the locations in which they occurred renewed interest in McInyre's original report from 1957, especially given other events that were happening at the time. In the weeks prior to June 18, three sheep and two calves had been killed at local farms, another heifer had been seriously clawed, and several dogs had gone missing. An article in the *Hartford Courant* noted that the slain animals had claw marks and that nearby tracks in the mud were too large for a lynx or bobcat.

Local residents began to speculate about the identity of the creature. Some suggested that it was a cryptid come down from Maine. Others debated whether it was canine or feline. Groper, who would have presumably known the difference given his profession, insisted it was the latter.

On June 29, a young cow was killed about two miles from where Groper's sighting occurred. The dead animal had claw marks on its back and flank; its neck was completely chewed out. Another cow had had its tail bitten clean off. Both cows were owned by Darwin Hughes, who reported that his herd had stampeded twice in the past month. The cows, he said, were also afraid to eat near the waterhole where the killing had occurred. "Them seem to drink and run," Hughes told the *Courant.* "There's something there waiting for them."

As June passed into July, Granby residents organized a hunt to try and catch the creature. Evidence from the killings was sent to the University of Connecticut for analysis, and local officials asked the state dog warden for assistance.

Youngsters got in on the excitement by hanging up hand-drawn "Wanted" posters. Adults, though, remained worried. They insisted that doors and windows be locked at night, and reported strange noises and nervous pets.

Emboldened, perhaps, by its success so far, the creature began expanding its range. On July 5, it was spotted by at least four people in Simsbury, who described it as lean and "coal black." Larry Graham, a 12-year-old boy, startled the creature while playing with a ball in his backyard. He showed police a book about panthers and said that was what he had seen.

Two more hunts occurred. Both came up empty, and the debate raged on. A local conservation officer insisted that the killings had been perpetrated by a pack of wild dogs. Other experts suggested that the animal's behavior was not that of a panther. Even State Fish and Game Director Lyle G. Thorpe weighed in, saying that he would eat a panther steak if the animal was caught and turned out to be a large cat.

On July 17, the creature moved again, this time to Barkhamsted. Two brothers fired at the "phantom marauder" when it was spotted stalking waterfowl at Windswept Acres Farm. None of the bullets found their mark, but the brothers were able to follow their prey with a rifle scope. They insisted that it looked and moved like a panther.

Later that night came a significant breakthrough. Dr. Robert J. Stadler, the owner of Windswept Acres and a veterinarian by profession, spotted the creature again and found that it had left prints in the damp earth. Castings of the tracks were made and sent to New York State Zoologist Dr. Ralph Palmer for analysis. Palmer confirmed once and for all that the tracks made on Stadler's property were those of a large cat. At four-and-a-half inches long and four inches wide, Palmer opined that the tracks had not been made by a lynx or bobcat, but declined to offer another explanation. Stadler further noted that droppings and vomit found near the tracks indicated that the creature may have been ill.

And then the killings suddenly stopped. Following the incident at Stadler's farm, things became quiet again. In March 1960, Dog Warden Groper submitted a bill to the town of Granby for 16 hours labor in tracking down leads on the "killer cat" and providing assistance to state officials who had helped with the investigation. The state had subsequently closed the case. Their final determination? That the killings were the work of wild dogs.

However, the "killer cat" would have the last laugh. Less than two months later, on May 9, 1960, the creature was spotted one final time in Barkhamsted. Howard Baldwin was walking his German Shepherd when he saw a 70-80 pound "short-haired cat" with a "long, thin tail" near his garage. After eating the food that had been left for Baldwin's three housecats, the large cat "stalked slowly off into the night" and was not seen again.

Observations

People who saw the "killer cat" provided similar descriptions of its appearance, especially with regard to its tail. This is likely because many mountain lion sightings are written off as people having mistakenly seen a bobcat or lynx. While bobcats and lynxes are bigger than housecats, they are also easily identified by their short, stubby tails. Most witnesses who saw the "killer cat" said that it had a long, thin tail. Others pointed out the shape of its ears or the color of its coat.

Then there were the sounds it made. While some instances were certainly the work of pranksters, many people reported hearing strange screams or cries during the height of the hysteria. Notably, the Simsbury sightings on July 5, 1959, were preceded by a family being awoken by roars early in the morning.

As in other cryptid stories of this nature, an "unnamed hunter" allegedly killed the beast and consigned it to an unmarked grave in the woods. Another person claimed to have delivered the creature to a taxidermist in Massachusetts, but when a state game warden visited the shop, the taxidermist explained that he had been given an Angora cat.

Given the observations by Dr. Robert Stadler that the creature may have been ill, it's conceivable that the "killer cat" is now, sadly, extinct.

The Killer Cat

Cryptid Category: Terrestrial

Notes: Val and I have our suspicions that the so-called "Killer Cat" was unjustly maligned in the press. As cat owners ourselves, we know — wait, what was that noise...?

*Barkhamsted, Colebrook,
New Hartford & Winchester*

The Winsted Wildman

It was a late summer day in August 1895 when Winchester Selectman Riley W. Smith was walking with his bulldog to Colebrook. Given the fine weather, Smith was going at a leisurely pace, meandering through the fields and picking wild berries as he went.

Suddenly, Smith's dog began whining in alarm and sought refuge between the legs of its owner. Before Smith could guess at the source of his dog's distress, a large creature covered in hair burst from the bushes. The selectman barely had time to glimpse the beast before it disappeared again into the woods with a fearful cry.

Thus was born the legend of the Winsted Wildman, one of Connecticut's most famous cryptids. From these humble beginnings grew a story that spread across the nation and continues to fuel sightings to this day.

Riley's encounter with the Wildman stoked breathless newspaper reports that began in the Winsted area of Winchester and soon spread to New Haven, New York, and Boston. The *Winsted Herald* published a follow-up on Aug. 28 in which Smith stood by his initial claim. Reports of more sightings by area residents followed in later weeks.

On Sept. 4, the *Boston Journal* published an article titled "Reign of Terror" that chronicled some of the Wildman's activities. Among others, the creature was seen pulling up trees, killing sheep, and trapping a woman on the roof of her home. Some speculated that the Wildman was actually an escaped gorilla, while others suggested that it was a fleeing convict or institutional patient. These theories seemed to pay off when, in October 1895, a tramp named Dennis Rippitt was "identified" as the Wildman and sentenced to two years in state prison for stealing from local farmers and other "depredations."

Skeptics have suggested that the entire episode was invented by Louis T. Stone, a journalist for the Winsted papers. Stone, they say, was a known teller of tall tales who fabricated the Wildman story during a slow news period to sell more papers. It just so happened that the story spun out of Stone's control when it was picked up by other news outlets and the Associated Press wire service. However, these skeptics fail to account for how often the Wildman was sighted after the initial hysteria in the 1890s and even in the decades after Stone's death in 1933.

For example, *The Evening Times* of Washington, D.C., reported on Nov. 7, 1898, that the Wildman had again been spotted in Winsted. This time, there was speculation that the sightings were a dastardly ruse to keep frightened people away from the polls on Election Day, Nov. 8. However, a stagecoach driver named John G. Hall said that he had seen the Wildman twice while on his regular route between Massachusetts and Connecticut.

In 1929, Frank L. Wentworth published a book titled *The Winsted Wildman and Other Tales*, chronicling the original story of the Wildman and how sightings and stories still

impacted the town more than 30 years later. One anecdote suggested that an uncouth woman "wearing a man's coat and smoking a pipe" was one of the "freaks" for which the area had become known.

These episodes were followed by a long period of inactivity on the part of the Wildman. That all changed, though, in 1972 when the creature was sighted again. In the early morning hours of July 24, Wayne Hall and David Chapman were up chatting at Chapman's house when they spotted the Wildman in the wooded area near Crystal Lake. The two watched the creature go into and out of the woods for nearly 45 minutes before it headed back toward the water. Hall and Chapman also said they heard strange noises prior to the Wildman's appearance.

Two years later, on Sept. 27, 1974, the Wildman was spotted once again at Rugg Brook Reservoir, just a stone's throw northwest of Crystal Lake. The Wildman frightened two couples who had gone up to the reservoir to park, prompting them to flag down a police officer on Main Street. Patrolman George Corso returned to the scene of the encounter, and though one of the men claimed to see the creature again, Corso did not catch sight of it. Dawn revealed no tracks or other evidence of the Wildman's passing.

There have been no official sightings of the Wildman in the five decades since, but interest in the creature remains. Newspapers throughout the state periodically run articles about the legend, while cryptozoologists, folklorists, and historical societies often given presentations on the topic. Don't forget also that it was nearly 80 years between when Riley Smith first saw the Wildman and when the creature reappeared to Wayne Hall and David Chapman. Going by this periodicity, we may have to wait until the 2050s to get our next glimpse of the elusive Winsted Wildman.

Observations

Descriptions of the Winsted Wildman are nearly as varied as the encounters themselves, so let's start with where they converge. Most agree that the Wildman is between six and eight feet tall, and weighs up to 300 pounds. It walks upright on two legs, is covered in hair, and is brawny and muscular. In 1895, Riley Smith suggested that he would not want to get into a tussle with the Wildman. This is notable because Smith worked as a teamster and "truckman," and was generally described to have an athletic build himself.

Many people who saw the Wildman said that it was covered in thick, dark hair. However, some accounts suggested that the Wildman had lighter fur that might have been reddish, brown, or blond. These accounts have given rise to the theory that the Wildman is not a Sasquatch but instead some variety of yeti. One report from 1898 even stated that the Wildman wore blue overalls and rags tied around its neck.

Though the Wildman has eyes that "swim in red fire," it also seems scared of humans. It groaned and ran when it unexpectedly met Riley Smith and likewise fled when it was discovered by the parking couples in 1974. Certainly, the Wildman is able to move throughout densely wooded areas quickly, though it prefers to stay near water as evidenced by the encounters at Crystal Lake and Rugg Brook Reservoir.

Reports from the 1890s tied the Wildman to the disappearance of small farm animals, which likely make up most of its diet. It was, however, also spotted eating local onion crops. During their time watching the Wildman for nearly an hour in 1972, Wayne Hall and David Chapman did not see the creature eat anything, but they did hear it make a noise that sounded like a cross between a cat and a frog.

Having been active for more than a century, the Wildman is exceptionally long-lived. It's possible that the creature hibernates for long periods between encounters.

Fun Fact

Writer Louis T. Stone, who first reported on the Winsted Wildman in 1895, is perhaps one of the greatest underappreciated cryptozoologists of the late-nineteenth and early-twentieth centuries. Among the creatures that Stone wrote about were: a cat that could whistle the tune to "Yankee Doodle"; a bulldog that brooded a clutch of eggs; a set of giant frogs that had a predilection for cigars and guarded Stone's summer cottage; and a cow that was so modest that she wouldn't allow her male owner to do the milking.

The Winsted Wildman

Cryptid Category: Terrestrial/Humanoid

Notes: Success!! We have just now collected this fur sample from the area of the last known slighting of the Wildman. To the lab!

Canaan

The Old Men of the Mountains

Hidden among the Berkshire foothills in the rural town of Canaan is a race of beings that the locals call "the Old Men of the Mountains." The Old Men are a mercurial lot — and probably not men at all — whose moods are dictated by how and when you encounter them. Meeting one is just as likely to result in good fortune as it is to being chased out of the woods altogether!

Stories about the Old Men date back to Colonial times. In most tales they are portrayed as being smaller than normal humans but not so small as to be considered fairies. A better comparison might be dwarves or gnomes, since the Old Men are fond of treasure and dwell in caves in the deepest part of the hills.

Even though the Old Men live outside of human society, it is not uncommon for them to traverse the wilderness or to even seek shelter with Canaan residents from time to time. For example, one of the Old Men once visited a local farm in search of food and drink. The Old Man said that he would be happy to pay for a meal, so the farmer's wife set out a bowl of corn meal, a cup of milk, a hunk of cheese, and a slice of pumpkin pie for her visitor.

The Old Man began eating at once and was so hungry that he made short work of the delicious food. Eager to be a pleasant host, the farmer's wife asked her guest where he came from. The Old Man, though, disappeared abruptly at the conclusion of the meal — even though there were no open windows or doors. The food and drink he had eaten rematerialized on the plate, and on the table were seven triangular coins in payment for the farm's generosity.

Currency of this nature is a common component of stories featuring the Old Men of the Mountains. Their wealth is derived from vast hordes of gold and silver that they keep in their mountain caves. From these precious metals, the Old Men mint triangular coins that are inscribed with strange characters and symbols. People who pay tolls to the Old Men or who acquiesce to their wishes are often rewarded with these unique and invaluable coins.

While the Old Men of the Mountains are happy enough to meet people on their own terms, they are far less tolerant of humans who chase them or trespass into their territory. There are stories of people who have caught sight of the Old Men, only to have them vanish before their eyes like the one at the Canaan farm.

It's possible, too, that the Old Men have some kind of mind- or reality-warping powers, since those who encounter the Old Men often do not feel like themselves. One Canaan resident who was out hunting in the woods saw the Old Men but claimed that they disappeared when he got too close. The hunter decided to mark the trees in the area so as to retrace his steps and investigate further. When he returned with friends the next day, though, all of the marks were gone.

Finally, there's the story of a man who ventured into the foothills in pursuit of a lost sheep. The man followed the sound of the sheep's bell deep into the woods until he passed through an opening in the rocks. Instead of coming out the other side, the man found himself in a brightly lit room hewn from stone. In the center of the room was a table stacked with silver and gold. Thinking, no doubt, that he could buy many sheep with his newfound bounty, the man began loading his pockets with treasure.

Suddenly, three of the Old Men appeared. They were angry that the man was taking their gold and urged him to leave empty handed. The man fled and soon located his missing sheep. However, the passage where he had entered the treasure room was gone, and he could never find any trace of it again.

Observations

The Old Men of the Mountains are often described as a race of "little people" but are clearly not as small as the wall-dwelling elves of Cheshire (see page 73), nor the miniature villagers of Middlebury (page 78). After all, the Old Man who visited the Canaan farm was able to eat and drink out of human-sized dishes, and the man with the missing sheep was able to enter the door to the Old Men's treasure room with little difficulty. For this reason, it is safe to assume that the Old Men of the Mountains are a distinct species of little people who grow to about four feet in height.

We also know that the Old Men are fond of wearing flowing gray robes and are adept at working metal. This is, after all, how the Old Men make their unique triangular currency.

Some suspect that the nineteenth-century writer Washington Irving was aware of the existence of these beings and wrote about them in his famous story, "Rip Van Winkle." Set in the Catskills to the west, which Irving describes as "fairy mountains," the story follows work-adverse Rip Van Winkle as he hikes in the woods to escape his nagging wife. It isn't long before Rip encounters a stranger whom Irving describes as "a short square-built old fellow, with thick bushy hair, and a grizzled beard." Rip helps the stranger lug a keg of liquor up the mountain. Their destination — a "cleft, between lofty rocks" — is not unlike the room discovered by the man with the missing sheep.

Once through the passage, Rip and his companion meet a whole company of stout, bearded figures playing ninepin. They ask Rip to wait on them, so he begins serving flagons of liquor, making sure, of course, to take a few sips himself. Before long, Rip is passed out asleep in the clearing.

Of course, everyone knows what happens next: Rip sleeps for 20 years while the world changes around him. Upon waking, he cannot find the rocky cleft through which he had followed the strange traveler two decades past, nor can he locate anyone in his village who knows him.

All of these aspects — the place in the rocks, the "toll" of serving the liquor, and the magical aspects of Rip's encounter with the bearded fellows — are remarkably similar to stories about the Old Men of the Mountains. However, it's anyone's guess as to whether those in the Berkshires are the same as those in the Catskills. And while it's a good idea to help any stout old men that you may come across in the woods, it's probably not wise to steal their belongings or drink anything they offer you.

The Old Men of the Mountains

Cryptid Category: Humanoid / Fae

Notes: No stores or restaurants in the area reported being paid with triangular coins recently. I imagine that currency of this nature is not very comfortable to carry in one's pocket.

Roxbury

The Giant Bat of Mine Hill

Mine Hill Preserve, held by the Roxbury Land Trust, is an excellent example of Connecticut's industrial past. As early at 1751, local entrepreneurs sought to make a profit from the treasures hidden within the hill: first silver and lead, and later iron, granite, and quartz. Some of these ventures were so successful in their time that they led to the formation of a small boomtown nearby called Chalybes, which at its height supported a post office, general store, railroad station, school, lumber yard, and more.

Unfortunately, mining at the site did not continue past the 1870s, though some quarrying persisted well into the twentieth century. When the railroad stopped running in 1935, the population of Chalybes plummeted. The Roxbury Land Trust purchased 360 acres of Mine Hill in 1978, with another 90 acres acquired over the following decade.

Today, Mine Hill Preserve is a popular historical and recreational spot. Evidence of the area's mining operations is present in the remnants of roasting ovens and a blast furnace, to say nothing of the darkened tunnels and air shafts that expel drafts of cold air on even the hottest summer days.

Another thing that visitors often notice is the presence of bats. That's because the tunnels in Mine Hill are a

hibernaculum, or hibernation shelter, for these winged mammals. Grates over various tunnels allow bat species to come and go, while preventing humans from falling into their depths.

These grates, though, may be protecting the outside world from something else. Town historian Kurt Jovan explained that there has been a thriving oral tradition for many years about a giant bat that makes its home in the abandoned mine tunnels. What started as a cautionary tale about staying away from the mine entrances has evolved into a lively story that is told around campfires and at Boy Scout gatherings.

Given recent threats to U.S. bat populations, such as white-nose syndrome, the discovery of such a creature is of great interest to cryptozoologists. Bats, after all, provide copious ecological benefits, from eating their own body weight in insects on any given night to serving as important pollinators.

Observations

Very few souls have caught sight of Mine Hill's giant bat, but those who have describe its size and wingspan as prodigious. Like its smaller brethren, it prefers the cool, dark habitat of the abandoned mines and navigates the tunnels with echolocation. Though the giant bat does not seek out human confrontation, stories say that it will defend its subterranean territory against any interlopers.

The Giant Bat of Mine Hill

Cryptid Category: Winged

Notes: Mine Hill has some wonderful hiking, and the air from the hibernaculums is cool even in the height of su———

Val here—we're taking Pat to the ER... he sat on something sharp.

THE NAUGATUCK VALLEY

Ansonia

The Goatman of the Opera House

Climate change has had a terrible impact on creatures of the natural world. Could it also be affecting the entities of the *un*natural world as well?

Take, for instance, a paranormal investigation that occurred at the abandoned Ansonia Opera House in April 2021. Video and photos shot by the research team revealed orbs, apparitions, and moving shadows — all telltale signs of ghostly activity. But then the investigators caught sight of something they did not expect: the silhouette of a goat-like humanoid creature. Suddenly, there was a cryptid alongside the phantasmal residents of the opera house!

This "goatman" sighting isn't unusual for the fact that it did occur, but rather for *where* it occurred. That's because goatmen are not native to Connecticut. Are the effects of climate change perhaps driving populations of goatmen into the northeast?

Stories of goatmen have persisted in Maryland since before the 1970s. The most notable tales come from Prince George's County, where a goat-man hybrid with disparate origin stories preys on everyone from family pets to young couples.

However, legends of goatmen aren't restricted to Maryland. There have also been sightings in Kentucky and Texas. For example, the Lake Worth Monster is described as "half-man, half-goat and covered with fur and scales." This creature was seen by so many people in northeast Texas in 1969 that police were forced to open a serious investigation into the creature.

Now, suddenly, a goatman may have come to Connecticut as well, if that's indeed what was sighted at the Ansonia Opera House.

Built in 1870, the opera house was one of the finest stages in the Naugatuck Valley and could accommodate up to 1,000 people. Over the years, it evolved to host movies, dances, sporting events, and more. But as the building approached its centennial, time began to take its toll. It was closed for safety reasons in the 1970s and has remained shuttered ever since.

Given the history of the opera house, Jeffrey Gerry has a different theory about what was spotted there. Gerry is the founder and lead investigator of the Connecticut Paranormal and Supernatural Tracking Society (CPASTS), and the individual who took the photo of the goat creature in Ansonia. He believes that the picture depicts a satyr.

In Greek mythology, satyrs were woodland creatures with the legs and horns of goats, and the torsos of men. Satyrs were the male companions of Pan, who shared their physical characteristics. What's notable is that Pan — and satyrs by extension — were music lovers. Pan could play melodies on his reed pipe "as sweet as the nightingale's song."

If there is indeed a satyr living in Ansonia, then an old opera house would certain be the appropriate residence for such a creature.

Observations

Both goatmen and satyrs share certain traits, namely the legs, hoofs, and horns of a goat mixed with the chest, arms, and face of a man. From here, the descriptions diverge. Goatmen are described as being between five and seven feet tall, and weighing as much as 300 pounds. The Prince George's County Goatman is sometimes depicted as a lab experiment gone wrong. By contrast, the Lake Worth Monster is covered in both fur and scales.

Satyrs, on the other hand, are usually much more human in their proportions, if not slightly smaller. As woodland creatures, they can move deftly through the wild or abandoned places of the world and, for all their love of entertainment, are representative of the dangers that exist on the edges of civilization. In fact, the term "panic" is thought to have originated from the god Pan as an expression of the fear that night travelers would experience upon hearing unknown sounds in the dark.

The Goatman of the Opera House

Cryptid Category: Humanoid / Fae

Notes: I let Val talk me into doing a paranormal tour of the Ansonia Opera House. It's scary here! What was I thinking?!?!

Beacon Falls

The High Rock Serpent

For nearly 150 years, Spruce Brook Falls and High Rock Grove in Beacon Falls have served as favorite recreation spots for residents of the Naugatuck Valley and beyond. Starting in 1876, the area hosted a pleasure resort, complete with river boating, skating rink, carousel, croquet grounds, and more. There was even a trolley that ran from New Haven to Waterbury, with a stop in Beacon Falls, starting in 1906.

All trace of the resort is long since gone, the buildings having burned down or returned to nature, but High Rock is still a favorite among hikers. Located in the western block of the Naugatuck State Forest, it offers one of Connecticut's most enchanting hikes: a steady upward climb along the ravine to a pair of stunning waterfalls.

However, High Rock is home to much more than just beautiful forestland — it is also the den of the High Rock Serpent. This multi-headed beast resides in a glacial crevice, emerging only twice a year in March and September.

So, how did a large serpent come to live in the Naugatuck Valley? The story involves Toby, a former enslaved person who was instrumental in the founding of Beacon Falls.

Toby (sometimes spelled "Tobe" or "Tobee") was possibly a member of the Mohegan Tribe who was captured by Col. Ebenezer Johnson of Derby in 1676. Twelve years later, Johnson freed Toby, at which time Toby was eligible to own property. With help from his former master, Toby purchased a large tract of mostly mountainous land in the northwest part of present-day Beacon Falls, where he lived until his death in 1734. In his will, he left ownership of the land to Johnson's three sons and to another man named Timothy Wooster.

Toby and the Johnson family were among the first people to settle what would eventually become Beacon Falls. The mountain where Toby made his home is still called "Toby's Mountain" or "Toby's Rock," and one of its tallest spurs is High Rock.

Over the centuries, Toby became the subject of many stories. Several unfortunately include culturally insensitive portrayals of Native peoples. In one, Toby trades his daughter to white men for a quart of rum. In another, an unnamed Native American chief, possibly meant to be Toby, romantically pursues a maiden from another tribe only to have his advances rebuffed.

The outcome of both stories is the same, but they point to the origin of the High Rock Serpent. In most variations, the Native American woman is driven to the edge of the cliff and, whether by accident or by choice, plummets from the top of High Rock. After the woman's death, her spirit returns in the form of the High Rock Serpent.

This creature only appears twice each year: on March 20 and September 20, or roughly the dates of the spring and autumnal equinoxes, respectively. Those willing to camp out at High Rock until midnight on these two evenings may chance to see the High Rock Serpent or even challenge the

beast for its treasure. That's the other part of the legend: that one of the hydra's many heads is adorned with a splendid carbuncle, or garnet jewel. Anyone who is skilled enough to capture this priceless gem will be rewarded with fabulous wealth.

It's important to note that these are not Native American legends, but likely the work of nineteenth century white storytellers who frequently circulated tales about "doomed maidens" and "foolish Indians." However, Toby was a real person whose legacy not only birthed the story of a fantastic cryptid, but is also foundational to the history of Beacon Falls.

Observations

The High Rock Serpent is a many-headed hydra whose body is lithe enough to crawl into and out of the rock crevices that are scattered throughout High Rock Grove. Its total number of heads is a matter of debate. Some people claim that the serpent has four heads, while others say it has seven. Regardless, all of the heads are identical except for one, with is adorned with a red gem.

Though many of the world's larger serpents (i.e. dragons) are known to keep hordes of wealth, the High Rock Serpent's treasure is contained entirely in this one precious stone. It is said that the jewel is not only priceless, but that it will also bring wealth and luck to the bearer.

Of course, one must be brave and agile enough to take the jewel on either of the two days in which the High Rock Serpent appears. No one has yet achieved this feat.

The High Rock Serpent is not aggressive except toward those who come to challenge it. Those who wish simply to catch a glimpse of the beast in March or September are usually treated with indifference. For the most part, the High Rock Serpent is content to observe its domain over this part of the Naugatuck Valley.

The High Rock Serpent

Cryptid Category: Reptilian

Notes: This was one of my favorite discoveries as a cryptozoologist. To think that such a fantastic creature was just a stone's throw from where I grew up! No luck getting jewel at spring equinox; will try again in the fall.

Bristol

The White Wolf of Peacedale Cemetery

Peacedale Cemetery is a lush, well-maintained burial ground that abuts a wooded area in the Chippens Hill section of Bristol. While this isn't considered one of the more haunted cemeteries of Connecticut, there is nonetheless something extraordinary roaming among the tombstones: the empathetic cryptid known as the White Wolf of Peacedale.

The origins of the White Wolf are uncertain. Some claim that the wolf was once associated with the Tunxis Tribe, though this may be another case of white storytellers misrepresenting Native American "legends." After all, Peacedale Cemetery is less than 50 years old — a mere babe compared to some of the state's oldest surviving graves, which date to the 1640s and 50s. If the White Wolf was present before the cemetery was established, it likely roamed this area of present-day Bristol, but it has since made Peacedale its permanent home.

The fact that the White Wolf lives in a cemetery isn't the only unique thing about this cryptid. While coyotes are a common sight in Connecticut, wolves have likely been absent here since before the 1800s. Likewise, white wolves — also

known as "polar wolves" — are not found outside of arctic regions, and certainly not in the Constitution State. All of this adds up to a truly singular creature.

Wolves have played a role in folklore since ancient times. The Egyptians, Greeks, Romans, Celts, and many Indigenous peoples revered wolves as the companions of gods and the manifestation of one's ancestors, among countless other stories. That the White Wolf fits into this tradition is not surprising.

Writing in *The Ghosts of Chippeny Hill*, historian Judith Giguere explains that the White Wolf is "symbolic of stamina, strength, courage and the embodiment of freedom." Moreover, the wolf tends to appear to those facing a troublesome problem, a difficult decision, or a devastating loss. This speaks to the creature's powers of empathy, in that it knows to appear at times of dire need.

There is no other information about the conditions needed for the White Wolf to manifest, such as times of the day or year. Even so, if you're visiting Peacedale Cemetery and see the White Wolf, it could mean that you're ready to take a difficult step forward, either in the form of a hard choice or in coming to terms with personal grief.

Observations

As its name implies, the White Wolf of Peacedale has a stunning white coat with nary a hint of brown or grey. When seen at night, this can give the creature a spectral quality. Those who have encountered the wolf further describe it as peaceful or perhaps even lonely — not wicked or threatening.

The White Wolf most often appears near Birge Pond Brook, which divides the front of Peacedale Cemetery from the rear. People in mourning or emotional distress are particularly prone to seeing the wolf.

While the White Wolf is benign, it is best to leave it to its own devices if it comes to drink from the rocky sides of the brook. Rather than approaching the wolf, one should let the creature dictate the terms of the encounter.

Although there is no record of the White Wolf being able to "speak" in the literal sense, it would be wise to listen to any messages it may bring, non-verbal or otherwise.

The White Wolf of Peacedale Cemetery

Cryptid Category: Terrestrial

Notes: Visited Peacedale close to sunset. It is a very serene place and just the right kind of environment for such an empathetic creature.

Bristol & Plymouth

The Marsh Monster

On the border of Hartford and Litchfield counties, between the towns of Bristol and Plymouth, respectively, is the heavily wooded area that surrounds Old Marsh Pond. Sparsely populated and home to a series of challenging hikes steeped in Connecticut history, this part of Chippens Hill is located just a few miles north-northwest of Peacedale Cemetery. This is significant because a cryptid that is much more sinister than the White Wolf roams the area of the pond: the so-called Marsh Monster.

It's interesting that two diametrically opposed forces can exist in such close proximity to each other, but that is often the way of things. Even among the preternatural, good balances evil, and the Marsh Monster definitely falls into the latter category.

Before Bristol was settled as an agricultural community called New Cambridge, stories told of a demon that roamed the woods near the primordial marsh. This creature was rarely seen, but its handiwork was obvious: small animals missing, then livestock, and finally human victims. Often, the only sign of the monster's presence was its glowing red eyes.

The true nature of the Marsh Monster isn't clear, but what is apparent is that it gets hungrier in winter. This lends credence to the theory that the Marsh Monster may be a wendigo (or windigo), given its glowing eyes and heightened activity during the coldest months of the year.

Building from that premise, it's possible that the Marsh Monster was once a person whose greed isolated them from the rest of society, so much so that the individual had to resort to cannibalism to survive. This, in turn, cursed them with a heart of ice and exceptional longevity, turning them into the creature we know today. Now, the Marsh Monster is doomed to roam the woods of Old Marsh Pond until it is killed or until the blight is lifted from its soul.

Observations

The most defining feature of the Marsh Monster is its red eyes, which seem to glow in all light conditions. Stories about the creature tell of it being most active in winter, with heavy snowfall only deepening its hunger.

The Marsh Monster feeds primarily on small animals, like chickens and rabbits, and on larger livestock, like goats and cows. When it can, the Marsh Monster will snare a human in which to satiate its appetite.

Judith Giguere's *The Ghosts of Chippeny Hill* relates the story of a Colonial-era child who went missing after milking the family cows in preparation for the first major storm of winter. Though searchers were sent out following the blizzard, no trace of the child was ever found. The only clue as to what might have happened came from those who ventured into the pine ledges of the marsh. They reported being followed by red eyes and hearing ungodly screams.

Important Note

See the final chapter for a brief entry about other "red eye" creature stories in Connecticut.

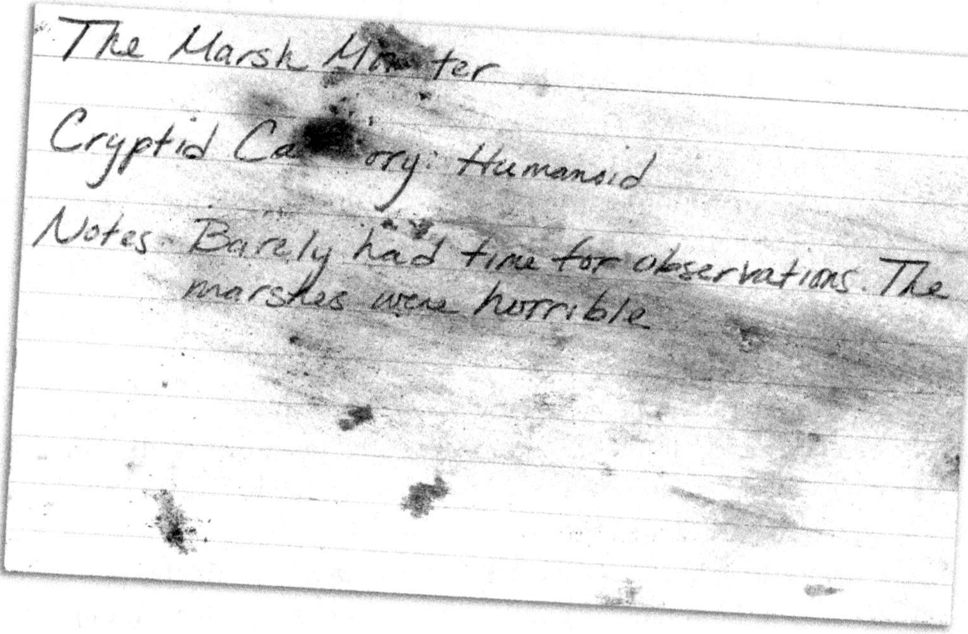

Cheshire

The Elves of Cheshire Village

The Cheshire Village section of Cheshire is known for its historic homes and institutions, among them St. Peter's Episcopal Church (founded in 1760), Cheshire Academy (founded in 1794), and the Cheshire Public Library (founded in 1892). With so much residential and commercial activity, this seems like an unlikely place to hunt for cryptids. Yet strange creatures do reside here in close proximity to humans.

We begin at the historic home known as the Hon. Silas Hitchcock House (among other names). Built near the end of the eighteenth century, this house was first occupied by Bishop Abraham Jarvis before being sold to Silas Hitchcock in 1829. It was then home to several generations of the Hitchcock family.

In 1918, Silas Hitchcock's granddaughter, Mary Dickerman, bequeathed use of the home, furnishings, and household staff to Mary Baldwin, founder of the Cheshire Public Library. Among this staff was Jane Smith, who had helped the Hitchcock family with cooking, cleaning, and other chores for several decades.

THE NAUGATUCK VALLEY

Jane, though, wasn't just responsible for domestic tasks — she was also the main contact between "the little people" and the rest of the family. You see, it wasn't just humans who lived at the Silas Hitchcock House, but also a group of small elves.

In particular, Jane communicated frequently with Vandi, who may have been the chief of the group or simply its spokesperson. Vandi often gave Jane advice, sometimes with a mischievous bent. For example, Vandi might tell Jane to leave the family's breakfast on the steps of the church across the street or to "gently" remind visitors when it was time to go home.

Not far away, at one of the homes on Spring Street, lived another creature of this nature that past residents of the house affectionately called Gussina. Built in 1850, the home underwent a full interior renovation when it was purchased by Dr. Fred Kramer and his wife, Sara, in 1976. Gussina helped with the revamp by unexpectedly pulling electrical wires through to the second floor. She also left antique pennies as gifts for the Kramer family.

Like Vandi, Gussina wasn't above a bit of mischief. She liked to appropriate Sara Kramer's jewelry (though Gussina always returned what she borrowed), rearrange things in the house, and occasionally shout at the family's housekeeper.

Observations

Owing to their small size, the elves of Cheshire Village are a challenge to observe. Jane Smith of the Silas Hitchcock House alleged that Vandi wore a red outfit and lived behind the sofa. This means that the little people are likely small enough to find cozy homes within the furniture or inside the walls. The latter would certainly let them move around a large house unseen.

In June 2020, the Silas Hitchcock House was converted from a residence to a professional office building. It is therefore unclear if Vandi and others still live there, given that the building is no longer a single-family home.

Gussina of Spring Street is the more elusive of the Cheshire Village elves. Though an article from 1977 describes her as a ghost, it's reasonable to suspect that she belongs to the same species as Vandi, given the home's close proximity to the Silas Hitchcock House. There's also the fact that Fred and Sara Kramer proclaimed not to believe in ghosts and therefore had "no explanation" for the things that were happening in their home.

No other description is given of Gussina, though it's clear that she had an affinity for shiny and beautiful things. Before the Kramer family bought the home, the previous owner related the story of a diamond ring that had gone missing for a year and had then turned up inside a perfume box where it was unlikely to have been stored.

The house on Spring Street has remained a private residence since it changed hands from the Kramers in the 1980s, so it's conceivable that Gussina or her descendants still live there.

Though all of the Cheshire Village elves seem to enjoy small pranks, they are never described as wicked. In fact, both Jane Smith and the Kramer family seemed rather taken with the elves' company.

It's also possible that these elves are related to the little people who reside in Middlebury. These creatures are discussed in more detail on page 78.

Important Note

The locations identified in this chapter are private property.
Please do not trespass while seeking out the elves of
Cheshire Village, as both the little people and the property
owners value their privacy.

The Elves of Cheshire Village

Cryptid Category: Fae

Notes: Despite the odd looks that we received, Val and I went all around Cheshire Village on our hands and knees looking for the elves. We didn't see any but Val did find this penny. Curious...

Middlebury & Waterbury

The Little People Village

Hidden in the woods on the Middlebury-Waterbury border is a strange settlement associated with another group of Connecticut's little people. Whether anyone still lives in the so-called Little People Village is an open question because the village itself has fallen into serious disrepair. Little folk, though, are known for both settling in unconventional places and for keeping out of sight. So, while the Little People Village may appear abandoned, it's possible that its residents simply *want* it to look that way.

There are many legends about how the Little People Village came to be. One story suggests that a man built the village at the behest of his wife, who was a witch and who communicated frequently with the little people. Another is that a lone man living nearby heard voices that commanded him to build the village. Still another is that the village was part of the Lake Quassapaug Amusement Park trolley line in the early 1900s.

Unfortunately, none of these stories are quite true. The village was actually built in the 1930s by William J. Lannen of Naugatuck. Lannen owned a gas station on the road between Middlebury and Waterbury, but when a new route was built in 1928, it bypassed the station and put the future of Lannen's business at risk. As a result, Lannen shifted use of his land from a service station to a nursery. He began planting trees and flowers that he hoped to one day sell to the public.

More importantly, though, is that Lannen also began building the Little People Village as part of the nursery. Writing in *Connecticut Magazine*, Erik Ofgang explains, "Using brick, concrete, ceramic and metal, [Lannen] made small houses, churches, a lighthouse, as well as steps and rainwater-collecting pools. Electric lights even lit up some of the houses." The nursery and the village grew hand-in-hand, and this may be where some of the legends mix with fact: a lone man building the settlement for reasons that were known only to him.

As the decade progressed, Lannen's plans changed — or perhaps the realities of the Great Depression made the idea of a nursery economically infeasible. In any case, Lannen married in 1936 and started working at one of the state power companies. By 1939, the village had been abandoned and was already falling into ruin.

But is the village *really* deserted? And why did Lannen decide to build it at his proposed nursery in the first place?

We already know that diminutive elves live just a few towns away in Cheshire, hidden inside the walls and furniture of at least two historic buildings. Could it be that the little people in Middlebury-Waterbury wanted to remain closer to nature and thus made their home in the woods instead of human houses? Did the elves personally ask Lannen to build them a community within the lushness of his planned nursery? And is the village still occupied today, its residents simply keeping out of sight whenever giant

humans come tramping through their land?

Any answers we might give to these questions would be pure conjecture, but there is one telling fact: The land on which the village lies remains undeveloped private property, almost as if it's being kept that way for a reason.

Observations

The question of the Little People Village is one that has vexed cryptozoologists for decades, given how difficult its residents are to observe in the field. Often, the only sign that the village is still inhabited is the presence of disembodied voices in the woods. Even these present a problem of interpretation, since the whispered words are usually too quiet to understand.

Like the elves of Cheshire Village, though, the little people are likely not a malevolent force. "Talking" to visitors may simply be their idea of fun or mischief, much like how the Cheshire elves enjoy "borrowing" jewelry from the people with whom they share their homes.

While much of the Little People Village is in poor condition, one notable feature is its elaborate throne. There are several theories about the purpose of this structure, including that it is used by the village leader or that it was simply a decorative fixture for the planned nursery. Some even claim that those who sit on the throne uninvited will be cursed.

Obviously, creatures of this nature are used to moving unseen. Whether inside the walls of buildings or through the roots of the forest floor, the little people are likely thriving to this day and we would never even know about it.

Important Note

The Little People Village is accessible to visitors but is located on private property. For that reason, Val and I can't give directions or recommend visiting there.

The future of the village is also at risk because of ongoing improvements and changes to Interstate 84 in Middlebury and Waterbury. As Erik Ofgang reports, the land could be used for construction, meaning it may one day be sold to the Federal Highway Administration or seized through eminent domain.

Keeping all of these factors in mind, please leave this little people enclave undisturbed for future generations of these elusive creatures.

The Little People Village

Cryptid Category: Fae

Notes: We continue trying to find a link between the Elves of Cheshire Village and the "so-called" "little people" of this area. Must consult with other researchers who have visited.

Naugatuck

The Nauga

In **1920,** the U.S. Rubber Company of Naugatuck, Conn., introduced what was arguably its most important product to date: something it called "Naugahyde artificial leather." However, it would take the company nearly 50 years to reveal the true source of this revolutionary material. That's because Naugahyde wasn't made through some fancy chemical process in a lab, but was instead molted harmlessly by creatures called Naugas. And while Naugas certainly did not originate in Naugatuck, it was here that they reached their peak fame from the 1960s onward.

To this day, one of Naugatuck's most famous residents was the inventor and chemist Charles Goodyear. Goodyear was one of the first people to patent the process for vulcanizing rubber and formed the Goodyear Metallic Rubber Shoe Company of Naugatuck in 1843. In 1892, the company merged with several others to become the U.S. Rubber Company.

One of U.S. Rubber's biggest products in the twentieth century was Naugahyde. First applied to handbags, Naugahyde soon saw applications that ranged from

transportation to theater seating. During World War II, the company also developed a synthetic rubber substitute that soon found wider use in clothing, shoes, and luggage. When U.S. Rubber became Uniroyal in 1964 and passed $1 billion in sales soon thereafter, people began to wonder: Where did Naugahyde *really* come from?

The answer, revealed on March 13, 1966, was the Nauga. Naugas, Uniroyal explained, were an ancient race of creatures that shed their skin naturally for use in the company's products. Rest assured, Uniroyal promised, that even though Naugahyde was sourced from an animal, it was obtained in a cruelty-free way.

This wasn't always the case, though. As more information about the history of Naugas was revealed, it soon became clear that not everyone was as kind to the creatures as Uniroyal.

Some cryptozoologists believe that Naugas originated on the island Sumatra, but archeological evidence of their existence has also been unearthed at ancient Roman sites, particularly near the Coliseum. Whether through the exotic animal trade or other means, Naugas eventually spread throughout the world.

Unfortunately, Naugas also became a favorite target for hunters and poachers — likely due to the creatures' docile behavior. By the dawn of the twentieth century, Nauga populations were teetering on the edge of extinction. According to Uniroyal's own records, "It was only after widespread newspaper reports of hunters aboard moving trains shooting Naugas for sport and leaving untold thousands dead and dying along the railroad tracks that public outrage brought an end to the slaughter."

Realizing that it needed to protect the source of its

Naugahyde product, Uniroyal in 1975 launched the Nauga Defense Fund (NDF). The goal of the program was two-fold: first, to build a ranch in Stoughton, Wis., where the company's herd could live peacefully and securely; and second, to establish hidden preserves throughout the country where Naugas could spend their later years.

Due to the secrecy of the NDF's operations, it is not known if any Nauga preserves are actually located in Naugatuck. Regardless, the creatures who share the borough's name do appear from time to time at community events and possibly even reside at the Naugatuck Historical Society's Tuttle House Museum right in the heart of downtown.

Observations

While Uniroyal advertisements often depicted Naugas as larger than life or taller than humans, these fanciful portrayals are at odds with the creature's actual appearance. In truth, most Naugas grow to the height of one's knee, though their rotund bodies and short limbs often make them appear a bit larger.

Naugas come in a variety of colors, which is no doubt part of their appeal to Uniroyal. That's because Naugas harmlessly shed — or molt — their hides much like reptiles (though Naugas are warm-blooded). These discarded hides have a variety of uses, and since Naugas shed several times a year, they provide a consistent source of Naugahyde.

A Nauga's color is usually offset by a "buzz saw" ruff around its eyes in a complementary shade. These ruffs cover their miniscule noses, which are otherwise imperceptible to observers.

Though Naugas have wide mouths full of sharp teeth, they are peaceful creatures who value limited human companionship. However, it is not wise to keep a Nauga as a pet. It is for this reason that Uniroyal keeps the location of its Wisconsin ranch and the NDF preserves confidential. For conservation-minded cryptid lovers, the company offers a program in which members of the public may "adopt" a Nauga. People who do so receive a doll facsimile of their sponsored creature to keep in their home.

Fun Fact

Both Naugahyde and the Nauga remain registered trademarks of Uniroyal.

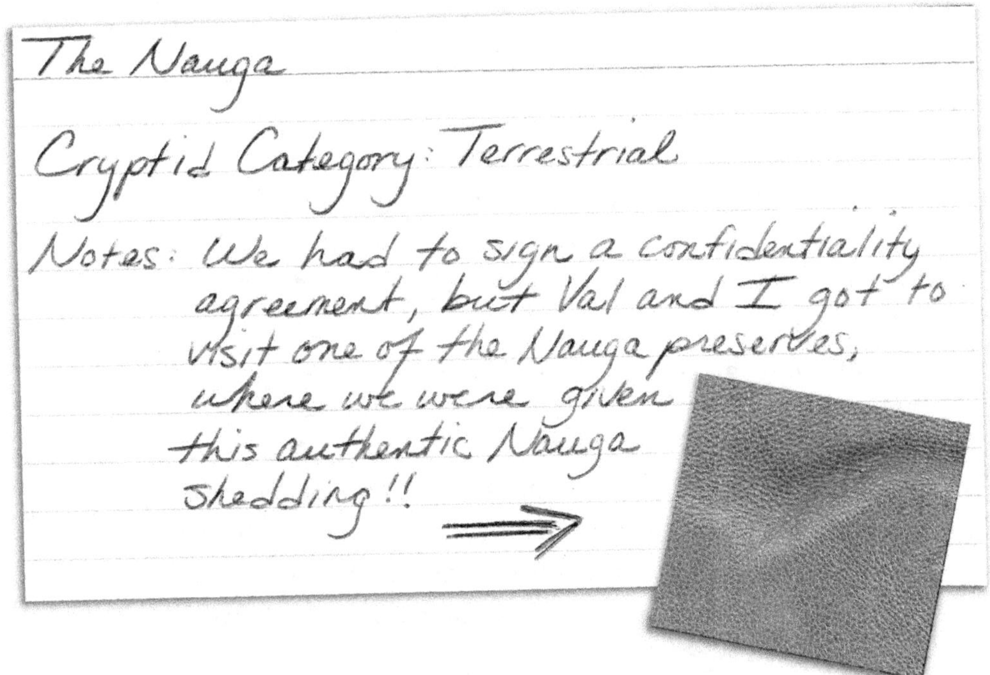

Plymouth

Buddy the Beefalo

The legend of one of Connecticut's newest cryptids was born in August 2020 when a humble beefalo escaped from a meat processing facility in Plymouth and set off on an adventure that captivated observers around the state and throughout the country for nearly eight months. Buddy, as the creature came to be known by the Plymouth Police Department, eluded multiple capture attempts while endearing himself to people far and wide. His shenanigans didn't stop even after he was eventually caught.

The tale begins on Aug. 3, 2020, when a delivery of livestock arrived at a meat processing plant in the Terryville section of Plymouth. Rather than go silently to his fate, one animal made a play for freedom: a one-ton "beefalo," which is a genetic cross between bison and domestic cattle. As the animal transport backed into the loading dock, Buddy pushed his way past the rest of the herd and bolted into the woods.

In the days and weeks that followed, police tried to apprehend Buddy while warning the public that he was "highly aggressive." In one instance, the beefalo made to charge at officers before retreating back into the woods.

Conservation officials from the state Department of Energy and Environmental Protection (DEEP) soon became involved, but to no avail.

By September, authorities were tracking Buddy using drones, and a local resident caught sight of the beefalo on their home security camera. Police, meanwhile, set up a trailer baited with fresh grain and made several forays into the swampy woods between Route 72 and Judd Road. Fortunately, Buddy was never fooled by these ruses. He would move away whenever officers came close and never ventured inside the trailer.

As early as Sept. 3, 2020, there were calls for Buddy to avoid slaughter even if he was eventually recaptured. Three days later, the Plymouth Police Union launched a fundraiser to purchase Buddy and transfer him to an animal sanctuary. The drive surpassed its $6,000 goal in just 48 hours, and the funds were set aside to send Buddy to the Critter Creek Farm Sanctuary in Gainesville, Fla.

Even with his future secure, though, Buddy remained hidden in the woods like "Plymouth's own Sasquatch," according to one article in the *Connecticut Post.* Rare sightings on trail cameras only fueled the beefalo's notoriety. Humorous signs in support of Buddy sprouted up around town, and a parody Twitter account was launched in his honor. Buddy even found himself emblazoned on t-shirts.

By December, police had redesigned the fencing around the baited trailer after several failed capture attempts, but not even the promise of a meal and a warm stable in winter could entice the elusive beefalo. In the end, it was simple biology that led to Buddy's apprehension.

On April 14, 2021, police announced that Buddy had been safely corralled — not in a manmade trap, but in a cow

pen he had been visiting at a nearby farm. Despite his eight months on the lam, Buddy was healthy and well-fed thanks to the efforts of a local resident who provided him with food and water throughout the winter.

But Buddy's adventures weren't quite over. After a quick trip to Massachusetts for a veterinary exam, Buddy travelled to his new home in Florida — where he promptly tried to escape again. Upon arrival at Critter Creek Farm, Buddy jumped the fence and entered a horse pasture. He was then introduced to some cows in a separate pen but decided that the female companionship in Florida just wasn't up to par and broke out of that enclosure as well.

However, a June 2021 update noted that Buddy had not tried to escape again since his second day at the sanctuary. He has since fully integrated at Critter Creek Farm, and the organization posts periodic updates about his progress. In one video from June 1, 2022, Buddy can be seen scratching his neck against a tree.

Plymouth Police Capt. Ed Benecchi, who led the hunt for Buddy, said he received calls about the famous beefalo from as far away as California, Utah, and England. Even several years after his escapades, people still post about Buddy on internet forums like Reddit and joke about starting a campaign to "repatriate" him back to Connecticut. Given this wily bovine's widespread fame, there is no doubt that Buddy has become a bona fide cryptid folk hero.

Observations

Unlike some other cryptids in this field guide, Buddy has been seen by many, many people, either on the web or in person. He is all black with white horns and weighs between 800 and 1,000 pounds. Capt. Benecchi also noted that Buddy is particularly agile for a creature of his size. Whether teasing his would-be captors near the baited trailer or prancing through the woods, Buddy is able to move swiftly and nimbly over rough terrain.

Though initially characterized as aggressive, Buddy's actions suggest that he was only acting out of fear or against those who were trying to capture him. Though no one was injured during the eight-month ordeal, there were several close calls among farmers, police officers, and staff at Critter Creek Farm. Still, the Florida sanctuary notes that Buddy has been content and at ease since shortly after his arrival.

During his battle of wits with the beefalo, Capt. Benecchi made note of Buddy's intelligence, as well as clues to his emotional state. It's possible that beefalo breeding may produce rare hyper-intelligent specimens, of which Buddy is one. If that's the case, only time will tell if more beefalo breakouts occur in the future.

Buddy the Beefalo

Cryptid Category: Terrestrial

Notes: Met with members of the Buddy Freedom Foundation (BFF), whom I discovered online. There are plans underway to repatriate Buddy to Connecticut. There is even talk among lawmakers of making him the official state cryptid!

Waterbury

Carrie Welton's Horse, Knight

Few **Connecticut cryptids** have public markers, let alone full-blown statues commemorating their presence. In fact, the Carrie Welton Fountain on the Waterbury Green may be the only one in the entire state. But the fountain's name is a bit of a misnomer. That's because it doesn't depict nineteenth century Waterbury resident Carrie Welton, but rather her prized horse, Knight of the Forest (or "Knight" for short).

What was it about Knight that warranted such a prominent memorial? To answer that, we have to look into the uncommon life of Knight's owner.

Born June 7, 1842, Caroline Welton moved to Waterbury in the 1850s, where her father was involved in the city's brass industry. This afforded Carrie a comfortable upbringing. An only child, she attended exclusive schools in New Haven and New York, and even apprenticed under several notable artists.

However, Carrie's first love was animals. From her family's home at Rose Hill Cottage, Carrie kept dogs, cats, rabbits, and horses. First among these was Knight, a black horse given to her by her father at the age of 20.

Carrie and Knight were inseparable. The two would travel throughout Waterbury in any kind of weather, and Knight

was lodged in a first-class stall that reportedly included velvet drapes and a personalized bone china bowl for his oats. Carrie was the only one able to ride the stallion, whom she outfitted with silver-trimmed tack.

Even though Carrie declined to marry, against the conventions of the day, the Welton family appeared to live in harmony until tragedy struck in 1874. On March 26 of that year, Carrie's father, Joseph, died after being kicked by one of the family horses. Was Knight the culprit? It's not clear. Articles from the time do not name the "old favorite" horse that was responsible, though family members would later claim that Knight was the guilty party while suing over the contents of Carrie's will (more on that in a moment).

Upon his death, Carrie's father left enough money to ensure that Carrie and her mother would continue to live comfortable lives. However, not even money can stop the march of time. Shortly after her father died, Carrie had to say goodbye to Knight as well when he was diagnosed with heart disease. She buried her beloved horse in expensive blankets and had one of his shoes gilded. This she donated to the New York SPCA, an organization she had come to cherish through her family's close friendship with the American Society for the Prevention of Cruelty to Animals (ASPCA) founder Henry Bergh. Carrie even had one of the trees at Calaveras Big Trees State Park in California named after Knight of the Forest.

For the next 10 years, Carrie traveled throughout the country, first to California and then to Colorado. She became a mountaineer and was one of the first climbers to ascend several peaks in the Rocky Mountains. Unfortunately, she also had a reckless streak that culminated in her death during an expedition on Longs Peak in Colorado in 1884.

And here is where we return to Knight. A longtime donor to animal welfare organizations, Carrie had two directives in her will: that the majority of her estate be given to the ASPCA and that $7,000 be set aside for the city of Waterbury to build a fountain in honor of Knight.

Of course, Carrie's relatives were furious. Two cousins sued to prevent the donations, claiming that Carrie was "insane" to have left that kind of money for the care of lowly animals. Fortunately, executor Henry Bergh prevailed in the courts, and the will was carried out as written.

The commission for the statue was given to Karl Gerhardt, a sculptor who had worked on several projects for the state of Connecticut and for Hartford resident Mark Twain. The fountain was completed Nov. 10, 1888 — four years after Carrie's death — to provide fresh water for horses and cattle.

There's another superstition associated with the statue, though. Watching from his perch atop four pancaked layers of granite, Knight also takes note of any humans who drink from his fountain. For good or for ill, those who partake of the waters are destined to remain in Waterbury for the rest of their lives.

Observations

In life, Knight of the Forest was a spirited black stallion whom only Carrie Welton could ride. During their approximately 12 years together, the two shared a friendship that was among the strongest between human and horse.

It's unclear if Knight was responsible for the blow that killed Carrie's father. While trying to paint Carrie as insane, her relatives may have suggested as much after her death. After all, why would Carrie spend $7,000 on a statue meant to commemorate the horse that had killed her father? At the end of the day, we simply don't know what happened to Joseph Welton in March 1874.

Though horses and cattle are rarely seen in Waterbury these days, the Carrie Welton Fountain still stands prominently on the green. Knight has gained a rich green patina in his more than 130 years but still looks ready to prance off the top of his pedestal at any moment.

Fun Fact

After Carrie's death, but before her body arrived back in Waterbury, rumors circulated that ghostly forms of her and Knight could be seen riding the grounds of Rose Hill Cottage on particularly dark evenings. The two had apparently been reunited in death to once again enjoy each other's company. And Waterbury isn't the only place that Carrie is said to haunt. Elkanah Lamb, a professional guide who helped retrieve Carrie's body from Longs Peak in 1884, wrote in his memoir that he saw Carrie watching him from the window of his ranch just two days after her death.

Carrie Welton's Horse, Knight

Cryptid Category: Terrestrial

Notes: While investigating the statue of Knight on the Waterbury Green, Val and I played a best-of-three match of rock-paper-scissors to see who would drink from the fountain. We've sworn to keep the "winner" a secret.

SOUTH CENTRAL CONNECTICUT

Bethany, Hamden & Woodbridge

The Downs Road Monster

Winding about five-and-a-half miles through the towns of Bethany, Hamden, and Woodbridge is what some consider to be one of the most supernatural sites in all of Connecticut: Downs Road. As the quiet street cuts its way through the woods, across Lake Watrous, and past Mad Mare Ridge, Downs Road abruptly ends in Bethany before giving way to an unpaved section of hiking trail. The road then continues in Hamden before ending at the YMCA's Camp Mountain Laurel.

Despite being home to picturesque landscapes and a number of beautiful New England homes, Downs Road has been the subject of persistent supernatural stories for nearly 200 years. The two dead ends that are connected by a hiking trail are frequently described as "eerie" and "unnaturally quiet," and everything from ghosts to cryptids to UFOs are said to be drawn to the area. However, all of these entities pale in comparison to the road's most famous and menacing resident: the Downs Road Monster.

To learn more about this creature, we must first examine the extensive history of this tri-town thoroughfare. The road is named for Samuel Downs, who settled the valley just south of Mad Mare Ridge in 1717 and is considered the first resident of what would eventually become Bethany.

Very little in the way of the supernatural happened in those early years. Downs Schoolhouse was built on the road in 1800, and Bethany Parish, which was then part of Woodbridge, was incorporated as its own town in 1832.

By this time, stories had begun to circulate about nearby Mad Mare Ridge. At first, these tales were about a horse that had gone mad and would let no one approach it. Then the stories began to morph into something more sinister. People spoke in hushed tones about a demon horse that lived on the hill, sometimes appearing as pitch black and sometimes as startlingly white. A publication for young readers titled *Oliver Optic's Magazine* even related the story in its August 1875 issue, describing how the creature was "... holding the hill as a citadel, striking terror into the souls ..." of passersby.

The article, though, also tried to debunk the myth, claiming that the hill was originally named by surveyors as "Madame Mère's Hill." This is a reference to Napoleon Bonaparte's mother, Maria Laetitia Bonaparte, who was known affectionately as "Madame Mère" (or "Madame Mother"). At some point after 1835, "Madame" was abbreviated as "Mad." while "Mère" was transposed as "Mare."

Another terrifying incident occurred in January 1856, when a man named Charles Sanford went on an unprovoked killing spree near the southern end of Downs Road in Woodbridge. Sanford murdered 70-year-old Enoch Sperry near Sperry Falls, then proceeded to the home of Ichabod Umberfield, which some sources describe as being near the present-day intersection of Downs Road and Brooks Road. After trying to attack a woman and child in the house, Sanford murdered Umberfield, who had attempted unsuccessfully to reason with the killer.

Thankfully, a party of locals armed with pitchforks and clubs stopped Sanford before he could kill anyone else. The posse bound Sanford and transferred him to police custody in New Haven. Though Sanford had a history of mental illness, he was condemned to hang for his crimes, but he died in prison before the sentence could be carried out.

As we enter the twentieth century, Downs Road starts to become a magnet for all kinds of paranormal activity. The presence of ruined foundations near the hiking trail has given rise to ghost stories about spectral children and disembodied voices. Some hikers note the apparent absence of birds and animals, while others report seeing trees move in the absence of wind.

And then there's the Downs Road Monster.

It's not clear when stories of the monster began circulating, though some point to the 1970s when Downs Road was a popular youth hangout spot. On dark nights, with the stars and moon obscured by a thick canopy of trees, revelers might see a creature lurking in the woods, or a parking couple might hear vicious claws being raked alongside their car.

As we pass the tercentennial of Samuel Downs' initial settlement, longtime residents of Downs Road know that the area is anything but normal. The part of the street that is now a hiking trail was closed to vehicular traffic in the early 2000s. As documented in a 2016 WTNH report, some locals won't even venture into the woods for fear of what they might encounter there.

Observations

Though Downs Road is allegedly home to a host of supernatural beings, the one of most interest to this field guide is the Downs Road Monster. And it's interesting to consider how the area's long history has impressed itself upon this cryptid.

For example, some stories describe the Downs Road Monster as a kind of Sasquatch with dark fur, while others insist that it is instead a type of yeti with white fur. Sound familiar? These are the same colorations used to portray the demon horse of Mad Mare Ridge.

Then there's the monster's predilection for stalking the woods, much as the killer Charles Sanford roamed the area on either side of Litchfield Turnpike while hunting for victims. Did Sanford's heinous acts somehow give birth to the Downs Road Monster a hundred years later?

Another item of note is the monster's size. The Downs Road Monster is often described as being shorter than its Bigfoot counterparts in the Pacific Northwest. This lends credence to the theory that the Downs Road Monster is actually a pygmy species of Sasquatch that is native to Connecticut and whose fur changes with the seasons. A heavier, winter coat of white serves as camouflage during the winter months, when snow is abundant and the foliage is gone. In summer and fall, the monster is able to cultivate a darker pelt that can keep it hidden from pesky visitors who find the hiking trail so attractive.

Like most cryptids of this variety, the Downs Road Monster is an elusive beast. It continues to stalk the woods with a purpose beyond human comprehension.

The Downs Road Monster

Cryptid Category: Terrestrial / Humanoid

Notes: We've been sitting in a hunter's blind in the snow for five hours hoping to catch a glimpse of this beast. Val says that she can't feel her right foot, but I think she's being just a tad dramatic...

East Haven, Monroe, Simsbury & Trumbull

Witches' Familiars

Though **Massachusetts** gets all the publicity for its infamous witch trials, Connecticut had its own witchcraft hysteria 45 years before Salem. Starting in 1647, Connecticut tried about 50 people for witchcraft over four decades and executed 11: nine women and two men. In fact, Alse Young of Windsor, Conn., was the first person executed for witchcraft in the American Colonies.

Stories of witches have remained in the popular consciousness long after the crime of witchcraft was removed from Connecticut's list of capital offenses in 1750. Neighbors might speculate about the arcane powers of a local spinster, while children might try to out-scare each other around a roaring fire. From whispered rumors to the classic Halloween film *Hocus Pocus*, people love to tell stories about witches — and a great many of these tales include appearances by witches' familiars.

But are witches' familiars considered cryptids? This was a question that Val and I struggled with while setting the parameters for this book. We knew we wanted to focus on creatures and animals, while avoiding ghosts and humans (with a few exceptions), but couldn't determine how to classify the three stories that follow. I guess you'll just have to decide for yourself.

The first comes from East Haven. In his 1836 book *Connecticut Historical Collections*, engraver and historian John Warner Barber related the tale of two unnamed witches whom he described as "the famous hags that were disturbing the peace of the land." In one incident, the witches made several hogs dance about on their hind legs. In another, one of the witches appeared to transform or otherwise share a connection to one of the dancing pigs, because when the pig's ear was cut off by a horrified neighbor, the alleged witch thereafter complained that one of her ears was muffled.

In 2005, professional storyteller Ellie Toy used the East Haven witches as the basis of a fictional tale about Goody Emily Anderson and Goody Anna Anderson. Among the Anderson sisters' menagerie is a tame, three-legged fox; an owl with one wing; a speaking crow; and, of course, several pigs. The climax of the story has a young boy finding the Anderson sisters and their familiars all dancing together — much in the same way as described in Barber's book.

The second story is of Debby Griffen, the witch of Simsbury. Debby lived a solitary life in the late 1600s, surviving off the wild fruits of the land and whatever small game she could catch with her rifle. When she did come to town for supplies, she often came with "exceedingly fine linen yarn" with which to barter. This is how stories of her strangeness began: The yarn was so exceptional that it couldn't possibly be the work of human hands. Surely, Debby had made a deal with some supernatural being to create such masterful fiber.

This wasn't the only story about Debby, though, and some of the others involve her familiars. Though she lived with several cats, particular note must be made of Debby's other housemate: a huge gray gander, or male goose.

The goose, which is not named in the legend, was known to strut up and down the property, "hissing and squawking at strangers foolish enough to come near." However, it's possible that the goose provided other services apart from "security." One autumn evening, two men returning to town passed Debby's cabin and watched as she exited the front door, leapt onto the back of the now much larger goose, and flew away on some unknown errand. It appears that Debby's goose was not only capable of changing size, but also of carrying human passengers.

The final story comes from Monroe and centers on Hannah Cranna. As a young woman, Hannah married Capt. Joseph Hovey. They had no children. One evening, Capt. Hovey went for a walk in an area he supposedly knew very well and fell off a cliff to his death. Afterwards, rumors swirled that Hannah was a witch who had not only caused the death of her husband, but would also curse any neighbor that crossed her.

Interestingly, many of the legends about Hannah involve animals. In one, she caught a man fishing in her trout brook and cursed him to never catch a fish again. In another, she caused a team of oxen to become immobile after two men stopped their cart in front of her house and mockingly asked her to perform magic.

And then there were Hannah's familiars. It was said that her house was guarded by snakes and that birds on her property could not be caught by hunters. Yet elevated above all of these was a rooster named Old Boreas. Unlike most roosters, Old Boreas was known to crow only and precisely at the stroke of midnight. It was even thought that Hannah and Old Boreas shared some kind of life force. That's because when Old Boreas died, Hannah predicted that her own demise was near. She died in late 1859 or early 1860. Her memorial at Gregory's Four Corners Burial Ground in Trumbull is a pilgrimage site where people often leave coins or smooth stones to mark their visits.

Fun Fact

During the 2023 legislative session — and almost 376 years to the day after Alse Young was executed — Connecticut lawmakers passed a resolution absolving the 11 individuals whom the colony put to death for the crime of witchcraft.

Important Note

Simsbury is located in the Capitol Region, but it is included here so as to group all the stories about witches' familiars together.

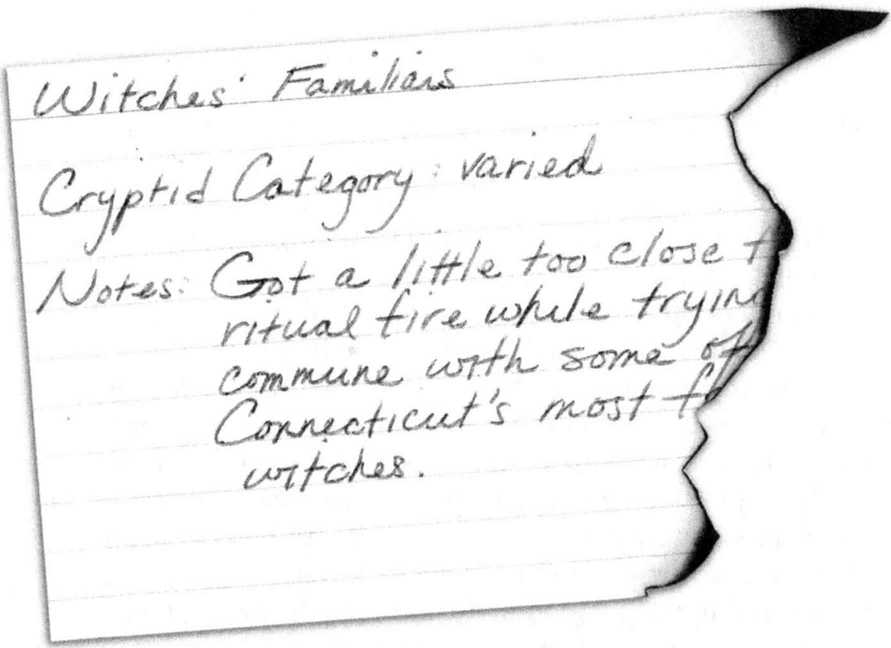

Hamden & Madison

The Sleeping Giant and Tuxis Island

Cryptids, by their very nature, are elusive, darting in and out of darkness, resisting capture by audio-video equipment, and garnering strange looks from non-believers. It's possible, though, that one Connecticut cryptid is in such plain sight that it is seen by thousands of motorists every day — possibly without them even giving it a second thought. That cryptid is the Sleeping Giant, off Route 10 in Hamden. But the story of the Sleeping Giant begins some miles southeast in the town of Madison.

In some Native American traditions, specifically the Algonquin and Abenaki, the giant Odziozo is known as a great builder. His name has several spelling variations, but it roughly translates to "the one who created himself." Among his works is Lake Champlain on the U.S.-Canadian border, which Odziozo made to foster peace between the native peoples. In one story, Odziozo moved the Green Mountains to one side and the Adirondacks to the other, and waited for rain to fill the space between. This became Lake Champlain.

Though Odziozo was a giant, he had very long arms and very short legs. In fact, he moved mainly by crawling or pulling himself along. In this way, Odziozo built valleys, rivers, and other geographic formations throughout New England. The fruits of his labor are seen as far north as

Quebec and as far south as Connecticut.

During one of his outings, Odziozo decided to follow a flock of geese to see where they were flying. In this way, the giant ended up in present-day Madison. Eager to leave his mark on the area, he lifted a section of land and placed it in Long Island Sound. This became Tuxis Island. When the resulting depression filled with water, it became Tuxis Pond. As an exclamation point at the end of his geological statement, Odziozo playfully placed a boulder atop another rock formation that is today known as Samson Rock.

From here, Odziozo's fate becomes unclear. Some traditions say that he returned to Lake Champlain. Others say that he remained in Connecticut. In either case, there is little doubt that Odziozo was tired after all of his hard work. Legends from Vermont and Quebec indicate that Odziozo settled in the center of Lake Chaplain to admire his work and to remind the native peoples of their commitment to peace. But some believe that he was too exhausted to have made it that far north. Instead, Odziozo only got as far as Hamden, where he lay down to take a nap and has been resting ever since.

This is just one story of how the Sleeping Giant in Hamden came to be. The Quinnipiac have a different version of the tale. Instead of Odziozo, it stars Hobbomock, another giant and culture hero. In ancient times, Hobbomock taught the Quinnipiac how to hunt, fish, and care for the land. Satisfied with his work, Hobbomock boarded his stone canoe to teach these skills to others.

However, things began to change in Hobbomock's absence. The birds, animals, and humans stopped speaking the same language. Strife was rampant. Hobbomock saw what had happened and grew angry. He made earthquakes so powerful that they changed the course of rivers. He also swore that he would punish the Quinnipiac when he next returned.

Years passed. One day, a young hunter was in the forest when he spied Hobbomock marching toward the coast. The hunter returned to warn his people, who pleaded with the good spirit Keitan for aid. Keitan cast a sleeping spell on the oysters of Long Island, which were Hobbomock's favorite food. When Hobbomock stopped in his travels to eat, he too became enchanted. Feeling a sudden need to rest, Hobbomock lay down and went to sleep. Disaster had been averted, and a new set of hills now graced the horizon.

Journalist and author Jason J. Marchi tells the story of the Sleeping Giant in his children's book, *The Legend of Hobbomock*, which pulls together several versions of the story into a single narrative. Amusingly, Marchi's story ends on a rather suspenseful note: Legend has it that Keitan's spell will one day wear off and that Hobbomock will be very, very hungry when he awakens.

Observations

Whether Odziozo and Hobbomock are the same being in different guises or separate individuals is a matter of debate. Their characteristics, after all, are strikingly different.

Odziozo is an ancient giant whose arms are much longer than his legs. He used his powerful hands to not only sculpt the landscape, but also as a form of locomotion. It's important to note that Odziozo was not *the* creator of all life but was instead a prolific builder. It is not known if he sleeps in the center of Lake Champlain or at Sleeping Giant State Park.

Hobbomock, on the other hand, is a giant made of stone — one of an entire race of giants that roamed the earth in ancient times. Marchi describes Hobbomock as having a voracious appetite, a booming voice, and a powerful stride that could make the earth shake.

Interestingly, the underlying motive of both beings was peace. Odziozo formed Lake Champlain as a diplomatic boundary between the Indigenous nations. Likewise, Hobbomock's role was to teach the Quinnipiac how to live in harmony with nature. He wanted the birds, animals, and humans to speak the same language because he knew that communication fostered harmony and understanding among all beings.

Important Note

These are just two versions of the stories of Odziozo and Hobbomock. Other variants exist, though I have tried to respect the spirit of my sources in retelling the tales here.

Sleeping Giant & Tuxis Island

Cryptid Category: Humanoid

Notes: Whatever is making the Sleeping Giant snooze must be very powerful since millions of people visit Connecticut's state parks each year.

East Haven & New Haven

The Fair Haven Sea Dragons

Just east of New Haven's Wooster Square, often regarded (correctly) as the pizza capital of the world, is the neighborhood of Fair Haven. Located on a point of land between the Mill and Quinnipiac rivers, Fair Haven has been a favored spot for catching fish and oysters since before Colonial times. Archeological evidence suggests that Native Americans began eating oysters about 3,500 years ago. The Eastern oyster is even Connecticut's state shellfish.

However, Fair Haven wasn't always known by its present name. In fact, it was once called "Dragon" (or "Dragon Point") when it was founded in the late-seventeenth century. Why? Because of the "sea dragons" that lived in the harbor and on the riverbanks.

Of course, we know today that the sea dragons in question are actually harbor seals, but it's amusing to imagine how these creatures must have looked to the first European sailors who arrived in Long Island Sound. With their awkward, undulating bodies and their loud, belching barks, it's little wonder that a pod of harbor seals could be mistaken for a colony of gregarious sea dragons.

What's truly interesting, though, is how much influence Fair Haven's sea dragons have had on the history of the neighborhood over hundreds of years.

When it was settled, Dragon was primarily an oystering community, and the Quinnipiac River was called Dragon River. As the years went on and the population of the area increased, it became clear that a bridge was needed to connect both banks of the river. When the Connecticut General Assembly granted permission to construct a wooden bridge in 1791, it was named Dragon Bridge and was connected to Dragon Road at the intersection of Quinnipiac Avenue on the east side of the river.

The original Dragon Bridge lasted for about 60 years, during which time things began to change in Dragon. The bridge attracted even more new residents and businesses, and in 1824 a town meeting was held to rechristen Dragon as Fair Haven. One theory about the new name was that it was inspired by Capt. Richard Russell, who remarked of the area in 1639: "The sight of the harbor did so please the captain of the ship that he called it the 'Fayre Haven.'"

Though the area and its businesses began to use the new name — for example, the Dragon Turnpike Company became the Fair Haven Turnpike Company — the unofficial moniker persisted well into the twentieth century. In *Fair Haven: A Journey Through Time*, Doris B. Townshend writes that the community was often called "Fair-Dragon" during the transitional period and that the wife of a local doctor was known as the "Duchess of Dragon" for her "grand airs and pretentious house."

In 1877, when a powerful storm damaged the steeple of Fair Haven's First Congregational Church, an anonymous poet wrote an elegy for the much-loved landmark, drawing again on Fair Haven's original name:

> *Into the port called 'Dragon,'*
> *Sailed a gallant ship one day;*
> *When the pilot, bold and fearless, cried:*
> *'Captain, we've lost our way!'*

Then spake the captain fiercely,
(His soul was filled with ire),
'Do you forget the landmarks?
Look for the First Church spire.'

'Aye, aye, sir,' said the pilot,
'I've looked and looked again,
And so may you, my Captain,
And own the search in vain.'

Over the next several decades, most of the land that is today called Fair Haven Heights on the east side of the Quinnipiac River was annexed by the city of New Haven through a series of complicated political maneuvers. The one-time oystering village, though, did not fully forget its past. In 1978, the motto of the annual Fair Haven Festival was "An Old Dragon with New Fire." The cover of the festival program was emblazoned with calligraphic swirls and the illustration of a dragon with webbed feet. It even included a poem written by Anna M. (Rossetti) Bishop. It begins:

In Fair Haven lives a Dragon
Who rests so peacefully
Under the Old Bridge

All of this because European sailors saw a group of creatures in the early 1600s that they could not explain.

Observations

Sea dragons — that is, uh, *harbor seals* — remain abundant today, and not just in Connecticut! According to Jim Knox, curator of education at Bridgeport's Beardsley Zoo, the harbor seal "is one of the world's most successful and widespread marine mammals."

However, this wasn't always the case. Harbor seals were

nearly hunted to regional extinction before passage of the Marine Mammal Protection Act in 1972. Since then, their population has rebounded to the conservation status of "Least Concern."

Though early sailors mistook harbor seals for sea dragons, their faces actually look more like that of puppies, with large snouts and whiskers. They also have dark eyes, clawed flippers, plump bodies, and sleek coats, according to Knox.

At just under 300 pounds, harbor seals are superb hunters who feed on fish, crustaceans, and shellfish. On land and under water, they are known for their barking vocalizations, which can be quite startling when heard up close.

Meriden

The Black Dog
of the Hanging Hills

ising over Interstate 691 are the Hanging Hills of Meriden, their sheer walls looming above the four-lane highway. As some of the tallest peaks in the area, the hills offer excellent trails and lovely vistas of south-central Connecticut. They also encompass Castle Craig (a 32-foot stone tower at the top of East Peak) and Hubbard Park (which was designed with help from the sons of famed landscape architect Frederick Law Olmstead).

It is for these reasons and more that the Hanging Hills have attracted outdoor enthusiasts since at least the 1800s. Whether for picnicking, rock climbing, hiking, or geology the hills have something for everyone — including cryptozoologists. This may have been what drew W.H.C. Pynchon to the area in the 1890s, for it is through his writings that the Black Dog of the Hanging Hills first came to greater notice.

Originally published in the April-June 1898 issue of *Connecticut Quarterly*, Pynchon's "The Black Dog" tells the story of a young geologist named F.S. who visits the Hanging Hills to collect rock specimens. Early on, F.S. meets a friendly stray dog, who stays with him throughout the day. The two travel the length of the hills together, and the dog even waits while F.S. stops in Southington for a meal. It isn't until after

nightfall that the friendly canine disappears into the woods again, close to where F.S. first met the dog earlier that day.

Three years go by. F.S. thinks back fondly on his day in the Hanging Hills and has a strong desire to exchange the sterility of his laboratory for the thrill of the great outdoors. He makes plans to return to Meriden for a late-winter hike with his friend Herbert Marshall of the U.S. Geological Survey.

On a cold, clear February morning, the two men set out for West Peak, well equipped with winter gear, rope, and a hand camera. They hope to take some stunning photos from the heights.

All is well until their descent, when Marshall stops in his tracks and points to a black dog staring down at them from the cliffs. As a frequent visitor to the Hanging Hills, this isn't the first or even the second time that Marshall has seen the dog — no, it is the third.

At almost the same instant, the snow and ice beneath Marshall's feet give way, sending him plummeting to his doom. F.S. finds the body of his friend but cannot retrieve the corpse without risking his own life. He instead returns to his lodgings to mourn Marshall's death. A postscript to the story notes that F.S. died in nearly the same place six years later, making him the fifth fatality to occur at the Hanging Hills in three decades.

In the more than 100 years since the publication of "The Black Dog," the eponymous canine has grown to become one of Connecticut's most famous cryptids. Many stories about the creature follow a similar narrative as the one established by Pynchon: Occasionally, people at the Hanging Hills will encounter a dark brown or black dog of indeterminate breed. The dog may decide to travel with them for a while, silently padding along and generally being a good boy. At some point, the Black Dog may decide to wander off on its own, or it may stay for the duration of the person's visit. It will then disappear into the woods when the individual is ready to depart.

It's all very innocent because "if a man shall meet the Black Dog once it shall be for joy." However, such a meeting may warn you off from visiting the Hanging Hills ever again. That's because there's more to the nature of this particular cryptid. If someone meets the Black Dog a second time, "it shall be for sorrow"; if they meet it a third time, they "shall die."

That was certainly the trajectory of F.S.'s experience. His first meeting with the Black Dog was on a perfect day that he thought of often when he became weary with his work. His second meeting was filled with sorrow over the untimely death of his friend Herbert Marshall. By the end of the story, F.S. is convinced that he will meet the Black Dog a third time and come to the same unfortunate end. We don't know with certainty that this happened, but we do know that the story concludes with an obituary from the *New York Herald* stating that F.S. died "on almost the identical spot where his friend, Herbert Marshall, met his death six years before."

It is unclear how many people total have died after seeing the Black Dog three times. Many reports use the statistic in Pynchon's story, but determining the actual number is likely impossible. After all, that's the nature of the Black Dog — no one survives a third sighting to come back and tell their friends about it.

Observations

Uncovering the true character of the Black Dog is difficult, since dark canines have been part of folkloric traditions going back hundreds of years. Here's what we know:

The Black Dog is generally described as a short-haired canine of moderate size with no distinguishing marks. Its fur is either some shade of black or dark brown.

Many who encounter the dog claim that it is unnaturally quiet and light of foot. The Black Dog is inquisitive but does not bark, nor does it seem to leave any mark of its passing. This has given rise to the suggestion that the Black Dog is a ghost. However, Pynchon's account describes how F.S. saw the dog's "breath rise steaming from [its] jaws" and how the dog enjoyed poking its nose into "every patch of woods" and "into every hole and behind every stump." These do not seem like the actions of a typical spirit.

Other researchers have opined that the Black Dog is a *barguest*, which is a large dog spirit from Northern English lore that usually foreshadows death; a *gwyllgi*, which is a spectral mastiff from Welsh traditions; or *moddey dhoo*, a large black spaniel that can be seen at Peel Castle on the Isle of Man. Certainly, some of the closest analogs for the Black Dog come from Celtic myth, where dogs are associated with healing, hunting, and death. Healing because dogs soothe themselves with their saliva; hunting because of their prowess as hounds; and death because of their instinct for carrion.

It's not too much of a stretch to explore how these characteristics parallel the three encounters with the Black Dog. The first meeting is one of joy, or a healing of the spirit. The second meeting is one of sorrow, or being stalked by grim tidings. The third meeting is one of death. It's also important to note that there is no "statute of limitations" between encounters with the Black Dog. Even if decades pass between meetings, you're still susceptible to whatever comes next.

Knowing this, it's easy to claim that the Black Dog is a "cursed" cryptid, but there's nothing to suggest that the creature is actively malignant. It's possible that we are instead misinterpreting the fundamental character of the Black Dog as an elemental force. Like death itself, the Black Dog is neither "good" nor "evil." It simply is.

Important Note

Even though it was clearly identified as a work of fiction at the time of its publication, many sources falsely present "The Black Dog" as an autobiographical account. The widely cited statistic that at least five people have died at the Hanging Hills after seeing the Black Dog a third time is drawn from the story. Many people even believe that the author, W.H.C. Pynchon, died before the story was published, given the way the narrative ends.

Unfortunately, none of this is true. Pynchon, who is the grandfather of famed novelist Thomas Pynchon, taught at Trinity College in Hartford and died in 1910 in Oyster Bay, N.Y. It is not known if the Black Dog crossed Long Island Sound to escort the elder Pynchon off this plane of existence.

The Black Dog of the Hanging Hills

Cryptid Category: Terrestrial

Notes: While hiking near Hubbard Park, I put my notes down for a moment to have a snack and looked down to find these paw prints all over them!

CAPITOL
REGION

Avon

The Talcott Mountain 'Robot'

As we'll see throughout this book, the line between cryptids and other fantastical creatures can sometimes become blurred. For example, are alien visitors considered cryptids? Some people believe so. And while this field guide doesn't focus on UFO sightings, there are a few notable creatures of possible extraterrestrial origin that have certainly left their mark on Connecticut.

It is not known if the Talcott Mountain Robot falls into this category or not. In fact, it's not a stretch to say that this creature may be the most mysterious one in this book for the sheer fact of how little we know about it. It has appeared only once, and whether it returned to its home planet or blinked away to another dimension continues to animate debate between cryptozoologists.

Shortly before midnight on Sept. 3, 1967, motorists passing over Talcott Mountain on Rt. 44 in Avon spotted a bipedal creature all in silver waving to cars from the side of the road. Police received their first call about the "robot" or "spaceman" at 11:30 p.m., followed by two more calls in the early hours of Sept. 4. Officers went to investigate, but a search of the area turned up no trace of the creature.

The following day, Donald P. La Salle of the Talcott Mountain Science Center was greatly amused by the

POLICE
TICKETING
AREA

sightings. "We live on a planet circling a third-rate yellow star off at the edge of the galaxy. Who knows what else exists out there?" he remarked.

After that, the Talcott Mountain Robot was never seen again. Whatever its true nature, it was content to leave Connecticutians with more questions than answers. Did the federal government sweep in à la Roswell? Was the Talcott Mountain Science Center ever searched to confirm that the creature wasn't being kept there for study? What did people really see that September night in 1967?

Folklorist Joseph Citro, for one, warns that we shouldn't be so quick to assume that the creature is of alien origin. Writing about the incident in the book *Weird New England* he says, "[S]o many people leaped to the conclusion that Avon's metallic visitor was something extraterrestrial. Maybe it came from right here. Maybe there's a whole colony of them hiding in the woods. And maybe if it had lifted its mysterious helmet, we'd have seen one of New England's many and varied crypto-critters."

Observations

Sightings of the Talcott Mountain Robot were surprisingly similar in their characterization of the creature. Reports said that the being was completely covered in what looked like a silver suit, including its hands and feet. It also appeared to have a reflective metallic hood or helmet over its head that obscured its face. Given that this was the dead of night and that the creature was only seen by the light of car headlamps, it's difficult to say whether the being was wearing a suit or if this was its natural skin or scales.

Though the creature's intentions were unclear, motorists assumed that it was waving to or trying to flag down passing vehicles. No one stopped — that we know of. Reports also said that the robot moved stiffly and awkwardly, perhaps because it was unaccustomed to Earth's gravity.

Fun Fact

The Talcott Mountain Science Center is still active to this day, offering a cutting-edge science, technology, engineering, and math curriculum to area students. Interestingly, the site of the school is a retired military base that once served as a Nike missile radar installation. Dr. Donald P. La Salle, founder, director, and president of the center, passed away in 2021 at age 88.

The Talcott Mountain Robot

Cryptid Category: ~~Humanoid~~ Cybernetic ??

Notes: Who is the Talcott Mountain Robot really? Why did it visit us? Did a passing motorist give the robot a ride somewhere? SO MANY UNANSWERED QUESTIONS!!

Canton

The French Paymaster's Spectral Steed

When one thinks of headless horsemen, the first story that usually comes to mind is "The Legend of Sleepy Hollow" by Washington Irving. Of course, that tale takes place in Tarrytown, N.Y., though it is delightful to note that the story's protagonist, Ichabod Crane, is described by the author as a Connecticut native.

While "Sleepy Hollow" has had an enduring legacy for more than 200 years, the town of Canton has its own lesser-known rider, whose horse is perhaps even stranger than the Galloping Hessian of the Hollow.

The year is 1781, and the American Revolution is winding down. In late summer, Generals George Washington and Jean-Baptiste Rochambeau will march south to confront British Gen. Charles Cornwallis. By Oct. 19, Cornwallis will have surrendered at Yorktown.

However, the war is still ongoing when this story takes place. The French and Americans have a strong alliance, and the tide of war is starting to turn. A young French lieutenant is on his way to Saratoga, N.Y., to deliver wages for the troops stationed there. Along the way, this "paymaster" stops for the night at Dudley Case's Tavern in Canton.

In fractured English, the paymaster asks for a meal and a private room. He eats dinner alone, then takes his saddlebags — presumably laden with gold — and retires for the evening. He is not seen by the tavern guests again.

About a month later, a detachment of French and American troops visits the tavern to inquire about the paymaster's visit. The reason for their investigation soon becomes clear: The French lieutenant never arrived in Saratoga with his precious cargo. Did the man abscond with a small fortune in gold? Or did something more nefarious occur?

As time goes on, locals become convinced that the paymaster was indeed killed for the riches in his saddlebag. Credence is leant to this theory several years later when a group of children supposedly finds evidence of a dead horse at Cherry Pond (present-day Secret Lake). While fishing, the youngsters snag the remnants of a saddle and what are described as several "unique" horseshoes.

Suspicion falls on the tavern keeper, who would have had a key to the paymaster's room and could have killed the French lieutenant in the dead of night. The tavern keeper, of course, claims innocence and is never formally charged with a crime. But nearly 100 years later, Dudley Case's Tavern — by then called the Hosford Inn — gives up a macabre secret when the building burns down in 1874. While searching through the rubble, workers allegedly come across a human skeleton in the basement. Some stories say that the skeleton's head was separated from its body, while others claim that it was missing entirely.

In the intervening years, stories begin to spread about a headless rider on Albany Turnpike. It is said that the rider is always heading west, in the direction of Saratoga, and that the eyes of his steed are alight with a strange blaze. Neither the rider nor his horse make any noise, but they will sometimes gesture in response to questions. Though the rider does not give chase or otherwise appear aggressive, those who encounter the being are often left frightened and chilled.

Though much has changed since the eighteenth century, stories of the paymaster have circulated all the way up to the present day. On moonless, mist-shrouded nights, wary drivers may want to take extra care on Rt. 44 for fear of an encounter with something other than the local wildlife.

Observations

As mentioned in the previous chapter, the line between cryptids and other entities can sometimes become blurred, and there is no consensus in the cryptozoological community as to the status of headless riders. Some feel that they are flesh and bone enough to warrant classification, while others consign them to the category of ghosts. It is unclear if Canton's headless rider is a spirit, but this field guide is actually more interested in the rider's horse.

No physical description of the horse is given prior to the French lieutenant's disappearance, apart from the detail that the remains at Cherry Pond bore unique horseshoes. This could indicate that French farriers were using different shoeing techniques than British or American ones at the time.

This situation changes, though, after the paymaster's disappearance, when witnesses began seeing the headless rider on Albany Turnpike. Those who encounter the horse describe it as completely silent, both in approach and when galloping away to the west on its unfinished mission. The beast also appears to have "eyes ablaze with a strange light" and is capable of uncanny speed.

In the years before automobiles, the horse would cause others of its kind to start or bolt. Once cars became common, the rider's appearance took on yet another facet. Lore suggests that headlights seem to shine through the horse and rider, but that both figures look solid enough that one would certainly want to avoid a collision with them.

The French paymaster and his steed aren't constant figures on Albany Turnpike and only appear under certain conditions. Foggy nights around the new moon are said to be the best times to seek this equine cryptid.

Important Note

Some versions of this story have it taking place in 1777, while others say 1781. The earlier date is problematic for a few reasons. Chief among these is the fact that the paymaster is almost always identified as a French lieutenant. However, France did not officially join the U.S. Revolutionary War until 1778. Prior to that, France *did* covertly supply the Continental Army with arms and ammunition, but only a few mercenaries — most notably the Marquis de Lafayette — fought in North America. Furthermore, no French units fought in the Battle of Saratoga in 1777 (though the Continental Army's victory there convinced France to officially join the American cause a year later). Given these facts, we have chosen to go with the later date of 1781.

The French Paymaster's Spectral Steed

Cryptid Category: Terrestrial

Notes: Val and I have been waiting for a foggy night around the new moon for months. The conditions must be absolutely right if we are to see this particular creature.

Ellington

The Creature in the Dairy Barn

n 1982, **John Fuller and David Buckley** were working for Valley Farms dairy in Ellington, covering third shift. One night in August, during the full moon, the two were making their appointed rounds when they stopped at the cattle barn to check on the cows. That's when they encountered a creature that papers at the time described as "Bigfoot."

As Buckley came around the barn door, he noticed that something other than the cows was inside. He immediately dropped to the ground, whereupon Fuller entered the barn and laid eyes on their unwelcome visitor.

"It was like something you'd see in a horror movie," Fuller told the *Hartford Courant* later that November. "The way it was looking at us — like a dog, all snarling and showing its teeth. He had his hand in the silage bin. I don't know whether he wanted to eat or whether he was just playing with it."

The men didn't stick around long enough to find out. They fled the barn and called the police. From there, it fell to Sgt. Frederick Bird of the Stafford State Police Barracks to lead the investigation.

Sgt. Bird interviewed Fuller, Buckley, and other farm employees. Though the creature had left tracks around the barn, rain washed the prints away before photos or a mold

could be taken. Lacking any further evidence, Sgt. Bird concluded that Fuller and Buckley had seen *something* that night — but he wasn't sure what.

"It could've been somebody playing a joke," Sgt. Bird told the *Courant.* But he didn't think Fuller and Buckley were the pranksters: "[Y]ou play a practical joke like that around a farm and you're liable to wind up dead. People out in the country have guns, and they don't like to see their animals spooked."

The evening after the encounter, Fuller's mother, Jackie, joined the two to keep watch, but the creature did not reappear. Jackie Fuller insisted that her son wasn't one to play jokes, and both men swore they hadn't been drinking. Still, their experience led them to become local celebrities for a time, especially when the sensational tabloid *Weekly World News* picked up the story in late 1982.

The following year, New Britain-based Bigfoot researcher Walter Brundage (who died in 2015) paid nearly $500 for Fuller and Buckley to take a polygraph test with a private investigator. The test indicated that neither farmhand was lying about what had happened. Buckley also revealed that he had seen the creature a second time about a month following the initial encounter.

After that, it isn't known if Fuller and Buckley had future visits from this hairy interloper. We know that Buckley saw the creature at least twice and that Valley Farms operated as a dairy farm until 2005. That year, the Moser family of Ellington sold the farm to developers, who razed the property to build the Big Y plaza that exists on West Road today. Even so, there are still plenty of other farms in the area that could continue to play host to this mysterious creature.

Observations

Bigfoot sightings do occur in Connecticut (see page 171), but there's reason to believe that the creature in Ellington was something other than a Sasquatch.

Most creatures of large stature are immediately lumped into the "Bigfoot" category. To be sure, the creature seen by Fuller and Buckley was large, described by the former as seven feet tall, hairy, and muscular. Its face had a flat nose and a mouth full of sharp teeth.

However, the creature's presence at a dairy barn indicates that it could have been some variety of brownie. Now, I know what you're thinking: Brownies are usually depicted as small or even tiny figures in popular media. In Celtic folklore, though, the term *brownie* represents a wide variety of domestic and woodland beings that can differ greatly in size and appearance.

For example, there is the *gruacach* of Scottish Gaelic tradition, which is described as a large, hairy, solitary creature akin to the wild man of the woods. There is also the Welsh *bwci*, another supernatural creature that often attaches itself to farms and domestic households.

In many cases, brownies are not malevolent. They are, however, otherworldly, meaning that their actions can be seen as mischievous by humans. Of particular note is that brownies such as the bwcïod often expect offerings of bread and milk. Failure to feed a brownie may result in broken dishes, spoiled crops, or cows being led astray.

That being the case, maybe Valley Farms had simply fallen behind on its supernatural alms when John Fuller and David Buckley were working there in 1982.

Important Note

Some sources indicate that Fuller and Buckley's encounter with the barn creature occurred on Aug. 23, 1982. The

Hartford Courant article from Nov. 26, 1982, does not give a specific date but indicates that it was the night of a full or near-full moon. Lunar calendars for 1982 show that full moons occurred on Aug. 4 and Sept. 3, so it was probably closer to either of these dates.

The Creature in the Dairy Barn

Cryptid Category: Terrestrial / Humanoid (Possibly Fae)

Notes: Walter Brundage was quite a famous CT cryptozoologist. I wish I had had a chance to speak to him about his discoveries.

Glastonbury

The Glawackus

The Glastonbury Glawackus is part of the holy trinity
of Connecticut's most famous cryptids, a trio that
also includes the Black Dog of the Hanging Hills in
Meriden and the Winsted Wildman. Starting in the 1930s, the
Glawackus has waxed and waned in popularity for decades.
Its fame was so great that it even had a foundational impact
on the sport of spelunking!

The "Glastonbury Wildcat" first appeared in papers
around Jan. 14, 1939, when the *Hartford Courant* reported
that a hunt for the creature would take place that very day
after sunrise. The county game warden organized the hunt
after residents had reported sightings of the creature for
weeks — not to mention hearing its "blood-curdling yells at
night."

Unfortunately, the Jan. 14 expedition was unsuccessful,
despite employing the use of a hunting hound. After
struggling through eight miles of snow, participants had
little to show for their efforts except a single fox. Tracks
indicated that the creature was large and likely "a member of
the cat family."

Within 24 hours, the "Wildcat" had morphed into a "What-
Is-It?" Reports in the Jan. 15 issue of the *Courant* opined that
the creature could be a mountain lion, a Canadian lynx, a

bobcat, or even an escaped zoo animal. Residents who had caught glimpses of the beast described it as resembling both a dog and a cat.

By Jan. 17, several town animals had been injured or killed, prompting a second hunt to take place that day at 8 a.m. This hunt, too, was unsuccessful, leading to perhaps one of the most famous headlines in the history of cryptozoology: "Guffaws of Glastonbury Glawackus Greet Gloomy Gang of Gunners."

Francis J. King, the *Courant's* assistant state editor, came up with the name on Jan. 18, combining "Glastonbury" (the creature's habitat), the word "wacky" (how the creature made people feel), and the suffix "-us" (to give the name an authentic, scientifically Latin feel). "Glawackus" would serve, King said, until the creature was caught and its true nature revealed.

In the same article, the county game warden once again floated the theory that the animal was a mountain lion escaped from a Vermont zoo during the Great New England Hurricane of September 1938. He assured local residents that while a cat of this size could prey on livestock, it did not pose a threat to humans unless it was cornered and starving. "That is, of course, if the Glawackus is a mountain lion," the article concluded ominously.

From then on, the creature's renown only multiplied — despite the obvious danger that it posed. As the Glawackus continued claiming the lives of dogs, a goat, and other livestock, the *Courant* kept pace with frequent updates. The Jan. 24 issue featured an "exclusive interview" with the Glawackus, as well as a full-page advertising section complete with a sketch of "*Monstrum Infandum, Gallonobacchus*" (presumably its scientific name). Want to turn your Glawackus pelt into a coat or scarf? Plasikowski Inc. furriers has you covered! Need to warm up after the latest Glawackus hunt? Look no further than Smith-Pearson Fuel Oil!

Sightings continued into February as Glastonbury, by turns, both feared and embraced its mythological mascot. The *Courant* published a map of likely Glawackus trails. Francis King offered to accept honorary degrees from prestigious universities for having been the one to name the creature. Good Will Grange hosted a Glawackus Dance Feb. 8, offering free admission to "anyone who brings a real Glawackus." And Glawackus tracks were discovered in Andover by Harold Roberts of East Hartford on Feb. 24. Even the Connecticut General Assembly got in on the hype when state Rep. Allen F. Behnke proposed a bill before the Fish and Game Committee that Glastonbury be set aside as a Glawackus preserve. (Unfortunately, legislators insisted that the Glawackus appear in person at a hearing for the bill to be considered.)

Finally, hunters reported catching the Glawackus in a bear trap sometime during the spring of 1939. News of the creature's death didn't reach the *Courant* until July 7, when the paper reported that the creature was, in truth, a large brown dog. "[E]maciated by hunger at its death, torn by brambles and fights," the dog was consigned to an unmarked grave that remains undiscovered to this day.

However, that was not the end of the Glawackus, if — to borrow a phrase from the *Courant* — that's what the hunters actually caught. No, the legend lived on, thanks in part to the growing sport of spelunking.

A decade prior, in 1928, Roger Johnson of Springfield, Mass., had begun exploring the caves near his home in the Berkshires. This hobby soon evolved into a passion, one that led to the formation of the first caving club in the United States. Johnson, joined by his young sons, set out to document the caves of New England with help from photographer Arthur Palme and journalist Clay Perry. Along the way, they assisted with scientific research related to bats while Perry began writing a caving guidebook.

Wanted! Dead or Alive
the 'Glastonbury Glawackus'!
Also known as the 'Monstrum Infandum, Gallonobacchus'

It so happened that the 1939 release of Perry's book, *Underground New England*, coincided with the Glawackus sensation in nearby Connecticut. Johnson, who was the son of a noted folklorist and who enjoyed a good yarn himself, decided that they should capitalize on the situation.

On April 1, 1939, the *Springfield Republican* ran an article titled "Intrepid Explorers to Track Down Horrifying Ectoplasmic Glawackus." A follow-up article the next day had Perry correcting the record on the nature of the beast. The Glawackus, Perry said, wasn't confined to Glastonbury, but ranged far and wide through its ability to become invisible. Nor was it a panther-bear hybrid; it was instead an unknown species that married qualities from dogs, bears, lynxes, and more.

Johnson, Perry, and their club organized "hunts" throughout the month to promote the sport of spelunking as well as Perry's book. A woman who was used as bait to lure the Glawackus at Indian Oven Cave in Millerton, N.Y., claimed that the creature had the tusks of a boar. Luminescent eyes and feet with suction cups were also added to the creature's characteristics.

During the final hunt on April 23, 1939, the Spelunkers Club of New England staged an elaborate death scene for the Glawackus at Bashful Lady Cave in Salisbury, Conn. Johnson "killed" the creature and had it stuffed. The taxidermic beast — made partially from a large, fluffy hand muff — was posed above a den of flat stones and put on display at the World's Fair in New York. Roger Johnson's son, Charlie, later said that the Glawackus lived in the basement of their family home for decades, and the creature continues to inspire caving clubs across the country to this day.

In 1966, a hoax in Essex that was meant to be based on the Glawackus resulted in the creation of a new cryptid: the Glowackus (see page 175). And in 1995, there were unsubstantiated rumors that the Glawackus had again been sighted in Salisbury, the town of its supposed demise.

To be sure, the Glawackus is firmly ingrained in Connecticut lore. There is a spelunking cave in the state that bears its name, as well as a camp run by the YMCA of Greater Hartford that focuses on nature discovery programs for children and adolescents.

Though the Glawackus has not been signed in a few years, it is only a matter of when — and where — it will turn up again.

Observations

Most popular depictions of the Glawackus show a creature the size of a large dog, with a thick, bear-like coat, and the mane, tail, and paws of a cat. These feline qualities would explain the Glawackus' exceptional night vision and its ability to climb, especially if it makes its home inside of caves. It would also account for rumors of the creature's "invisibility," since cats can move through their environments quite silently.

We also know that the Glawackus has the teeth of a predator, though it is less clear if the Glawackus has tusks, as described by one witness. It's possible that only one sex of the species has this characteristic, while the other does not.

Fun Fact

There is a popular theory among conspiracy-minded Connecticut residents that the state Department of Energy and Environmental Protection (DEEP) is hiding information about the existence of mountain lions in the state. Amusingly, this denial goes back to at least 1939 and the emergence of the Glawackus. Questioned that the creature may be a mountain lion (or catamount), the Connecticut

Geological and Natural History Survey (now part of DEEP) replied in the negative. Reported the *Hartford Courant*: "The authoritative 'Mammals of Connecticut' published by the State Geological and Natural History Survey, discourages the catamount theory; it admits that the animal once roamed Connecticut, but 'today it probably does not occur east of the Mississippi except in Florida and South Georgia.'"

Talk about playing the long game, DEEP! (See also the entry for mountain lions in this book's final chapter.)

The Glawackus

Cryptid Category: Terrestrial

Notes: There is so much to cover with the Glawackus — where do I even begin?! It is so important that we do justice to this critical piece of cryptozoological history.

Glastonbury

The Pterodactyl

One would be forgiven for assuming that Glastonbury is home to only one cryptid, given the outsize popularity of the Glawackus. Fortunately for those of us who study cryptozoology, that assumption is incorrect. While the Glawackus may be the dominant *land-based* cryptid in Glastonbury, there is a second creature that rules the skies above: a pterodactyl.

No one is quite sure when the Glastonbury pterodactyl first appeared, but we do know when residents decided to try and do something about this aerial fiend.

In January 1956, the Glastonbury Sportsmen's Association elected a new slate of officers that included Richard S. Potter as its president. Potter's first act in this new role was to declare a pterodactyl hunt to take place Jan. 21. "We must put an end to this creature or prove without a doubt that it does not exist," he declared.

At least two members of the club had claimed to see the pterodactyl at the Glastonbury Meadows state wildlife area, and their experiences led to them becoming squad leaders for the hunt. E.H. Tyrol was named hunt master.

About 50 people participated in the expedition, but none "returned with a pterodactyl skin dangling from his belt," according to a report in the *Hartford Courant* the following

day. Although a few members of the association caught glimpses of their prey, the creature remained at large. Of particular note was Herbert Clark's discovery of supposed pterodactyl tracks. In the *Courant* article, Clark is billed as "the last man to have seen the legendary Glastonbury Glawackus."

The failure of the hunt unfortunately meant that the Sportsmen's Association did not have any pterodactyl soup to serve at its annual dinner on Jan. 28. Described as the culmination of the previous year's hunting season, the dinner served as an opportunity for hunters to take their best "bags" out of deep freeze to serve at a community meal. "In other words, the interest of the members in the possible seizure of a pterodactyl is culinary, not scientific," explained Thomas E. Murphy in an editorial in which he went on to discuss possible methods of cooking the winged reptile. E. Robert Stevenson, a former editor at the Waterbury *Republican-American*, added his own two cents in another editorial. "After seeing Australia, I can believe in Glastonbury's pterodactyl," he wrote.

Notably, this was not the last time that the Sportsmen's Associated tried to serve such an exotic dish at its annual event. One year later, in 1957, the association wrote to noted newscaster and traveler Lowell Thomas asking if Thomas could spare any wooly mammoth meat for the 200 guests at that year's dinner.

Observations

Having never been caught, it can be assumed that the pterodactyl or its kin are still at large in and around Glastonbury. Those who saw the creature in 1956 described it as gray or brown with a six- to eight-foot wingspan and a long tail. The tracks discovered by Herbert Clark displayed one foot that was clawed and another that was webbed.

Regrettably, there are no reports on the nutritional value of eating pterodactyl meat.

The Pterodactyl

Cryptid Category: Winged

Notes: Found the Glastonbury Sportsmen's recipe for their pterodactyl soup. Ingredients:

- 1 lb ground pterodactyl
- 1 onion
- 5 carrots
- 1 ½ cup water
- 1 tsp salt
- 1 tsp pepper
- 46 oz vegetable juice

LOWER CONNECTICUT RIVER VALLEY

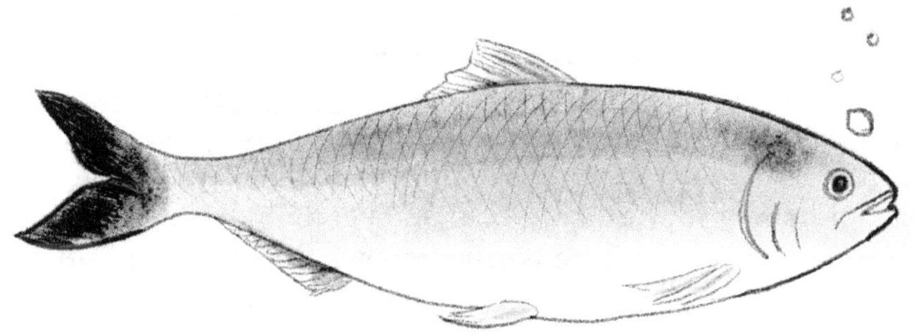

Chester, Essex, Lyme, Old Lyme & Old Saybrook

The Shad Spirit

To fair Connecticut's northernmost source,
O'er sand-bars, rapids, and falls,
The Shad Spirit holds his onward course,
With the flocks which his whistle calls.

– "The Shad Spirit" by John G.C. Brainard, 1824

For thousands of years, the American shad has provided nutritional and economic sustenance to people living along the Connecticut River. For Native Americans, this fish was an important dietary staple before the colonization of North America. After the coming of the Europeans, settlers began fishing for both personal and economic gain. In fact, commercial shad fishing has lasted well into the twenty-first century, though today's fishermen will admit that the trade is not nearly as vibrant as it once was.

Given the shad's historic importance to the Northeast, and Connecticut in particular, is it any wonder that legend tells of an otherworldly creature that comes to guide the shad to their spawning grounds each spring? Indeed, this is the role of the so-called Shad Spirit, which has been a muse for several generations of Connecticut artists.

Though the Shad Spirit is possibly older than recorded

history, its existence was greatly championed by nineteenth-century poet John G.C. Brainard. A frequent contributor to the *Connecticut Mirror* newspaper, Brainard wrote at least two versions of a poem about the yearly coming of the Shad Spirit, which he called "a kind of *Yankee bogle.*"

The function of the Shad Spirit is two-fold: Its first task is to guide the shad from their ocean habitats to the inland rivers where they spawn; its second is to alert fishermen to begin preparing their nets for the season. The Shad Spirit does these things by taking on the form of a giant bird. This is how the creature is able to fly long distances between the Atlantic Ocean and the many tidal rivers of the eastern seaboard, where the shad reproduce. This is also a possible source of the Shad Spirit's entrancing music.

Music is a seminal part of the Shad Spirit's journey. The tune that the creature plays is so irresistible that the shad are compelled to follow. While the music doesn't have quite the same effect on humans, it is still an important reminder that the fishing season is nigh and that preparations must be made for the annual harvest. Otherwise, as Brainard writes, "the nets would be swept to no purpose, and the fisherman would labor in vain."

Thus does the Shad Spirit complete its yearly pilgrimage, one that brings abundance to Connecticut's waterways just as the weather is starting to warm.

Observations

While the Shad Spirit's true form is not known, it most often appears as a large bird capable of long, sustained flight. It is sometimes described as a nighthawk or a Wilson's snipe. The former generally has a blunt beak and brown-and-white plumage with prominent white marks on the underside of its wings. Snipes, on the other hand, have long, prominent beaks, brown plumage, and white underbellies. Given the Shad Spirit's association with water, it may be closer in approximation to the snipe, which is indeed a shorebird.

The Shad Spirit's other notable characteristic is its musicality, which it uses to call both the shad and the fishermen to their purpose. Some sources attribute this to birdsong while the Shad Spirit is in its avian form, while others state that the Shad Spirit carries some kind of musical instrument. In Brainard's poem, the source of the music is a whistle.

As a fish species, shad and their roe are highly prized for their distinct flavor and high omega-3 content. Mature fish grow to between 20 and 25 inches long and have silver, green, and blue scales.

Those interested in catching a glimpse of the Shad Spirit must try their luck in the spring or early summer. In the Connecticut River, shad spawning season is generally April to June, depending on water temperature. The Shad Spirit appears about a week before the fish do.

Colchester, East Haddam, East Hampton, Haddam, Hebron & Marlborough

The Black Fox of the Salmon River

Comprised of approximately 6,000 acres of land, the Salmon River State Forest is a treasured ecosystem that has provided natural resources since long before it was ever designated as a state park. The area was said to be prized hunting and fishing grounds for Indigenous peoples, and later for European colonists. Today, the forest and watershed offer opportunities for fly fishing, sport hunting, hiking, and more.

Part of the Salmon River State Forest's popularity comes from its abundance of fish and game, which include trout, small mammals, pheasant, waterfowl, wild turkey, and deer. However, one creature in the forest is prized above all else: the Black Fox. That this crafty cryptid is seemingly impossible to catch has only added to its allure for nearly 400 years.

Stories of mythical black foxes are not unique to Connecticut. In 1643, Roger Williams of Rhode Island wrote about such creatures in his seminal book, *A Key into the Language of America*. Williams explained, "The *Indians* say they have black Foxes, which they have often seene, but never could take any of them: they say they are *Manittóoes*, that is, God's Spirits or Divine powers ..."

The origin of Connecticut's particular fox is not clear. Some sources suggest that the Black Fox of the Salmon River sprang from Native American tales, but there is also evidence that the story was romanticized by white writers. That is certainly the case with two nineteenth-century poets, who brought the Black Fox to wider audiences while mixing sources of Indigenous lore for their own narrative purposes.

John G.C. Brainard, who also wrote about the Shad Spirit (see previous chapter), mentions the Black Fox in both an ode to the Salmon River and in an 1824 poem in which the fox is the main subject. In his telling, the Salmon River was a mystical spot for Native American shamans and chiefs to seek counsel.

Likewise, John Greenleaf Whittier, who admired Brainard's work, expounded on the Black Fox in his own poem from 1831. Whittier wrote of the eponymous creature:

A hunter like my father then
We never more shall see —
The mountain-cat was not more swift
Of eye and foot than he:
His aim was fatal in the air
And on the tallest tree,

> *Yet close beneath his ready aim*
> *The Black Fox hurried on,*
> *And when the forest echoes mocked*
> *The sharp voice of his gun,*
> *The creature gave a frightful yell,*
> *Long, loud, but only one.*

Whittier's work, which is significantly longer than both of Brainard's poems combined, strikes at the heart of what makes the Black Fox so alluring: namely, that no weapon made by human hands can seemingly harm the creature. As countless hunters have learned throughout the years, arrows, musket balls, and bullets all seem to miss their intended target. The fox merely continues on its way, daring the hunter to follow — and whether through conscious choice or something more ethereal, this usually happens.

Despite the seemingly insurmountable obstacle of the fox's invulnerability, one glimpse of the creature is usually enough to compel a hunter to track the Black Fox until the hunter is on the brink of exhaustion or even death. Those who are able to break free from the trance arrive home drained and starving. Those who aren't are never seen again.

What happens to these individuals isn't known. It's possible they become lost in the depths of the Salmon River State Forest and die of exposure. Or it's possible they meet a more fearsome end — one in which they finally get a close-up view of the forest's timeless supernatural resident.

Observations

Stories about the Black Fox of the Salmon River invariably share one thing: the creature's coat. The fox has thick, lustrous fur of unsurpassed quality. This trait is what drives another part of the legend: that anyone who sees the Black Fox becomes immediately covetous of its pelt and is compelled to chase the creature deep into the woods.

The desire to capture the Black Fox is ultimately what leads hunters on a chase that can last hours or even days. Each failed attempt, each shot that goes awry, only drives the hunter to further lust. As poet John G.C. Brainard writes,

The hunters chase o'er dale and hill,
They may not, though they would, look back,
They must go forward — forward still.

Some cryptozoologists have suggested that the Black Fox is not a fox at all, but instead a trickster spirit of the forest who merely takes the form of a fox. This might explain why most weapons are incapable of harming the Black Fox. John Greenleaf Whittier opines that the fox was once a Native American chief who was transformed for some "unspoken crime." Brainard, meanwhile, wrote that the "Indian Druids" supposedly knew of a material that could harm the fox, though this material appears in neither summer nor winter.

It's important to note that none of these details are likely derived from actual Indigenous traditions but were invented in the name of making the stories more "exotic."

The Black Fox

Cryptid Category: Terrestrial

Notes: It is often wise to work in pairs while seeking cryptids. Case in point: I was the first to spot the Black Fox today and would have fled after it if Val had not restrained me. I just wanted to touch the creature's fur…

*Cromwell, Middletown, Old Lyme,
Old Saybrook & Portland*

The Connecticut River Serpent

From its source near the Canadian border, the Connecticut River flows 410 miles south through Vermont, New Hampshire, Massachusetts, and Connecticut before emptying into Long Island Sound. As New England's longest waterway, its tributaries form some of the other notable rivers in the state, including the Farmington River and the Eightmile River.

Given its length and course, it is little wonder that the Connecticut River has traditionally been an important avenue for travel and commerce. This was certainly the case in the nineteenth century, when our story begins.

On the morning of Sept. 8, 1886, Silas Sage and Col. Stocking set out on the Connecticut River from Cromwell at about 6 a.m. Both were experienced boatmen who had made the crossing to Portland and Middletown many times before. There was no expectation that the trip that day would be any different.

However, as they reached the middle of the stream, something struck their skiff with enough force to send the two men sprawling. Sage and Stocking quickly got to their feet and recovered their oars, only to watch in terror as the water nearby began to churn and foam. A loud noise filled the air, and out of the roiling river emerged the head and neck of a serpentine creature. Fearing now for their lives, Sage and Stocking paddled furiously to shore.

On the Portland side of the river, the men began telling their story to others nearby. The tale was initially met with skepticism — until the creature appeared a second time. To the astonishment of onlookers, the beast rose 15 feet out of the water before speeding upriver and disappearing near Gildersleeve Island.

With the river community now on high alert, armed citizens kept watch from the shore while "all available boats were pressed into service" to search the water. Unfortunately, the serpent did not appear again, at least in that part of the river.

Two years later, in 1888, Capt. Sherman of the schooner *Coral* spotted the creature gliding across the surface of the water near the mouth of the Connecticut River between Old Saybrook and Old Lyme. Sherman called to his mate, who also saw the hundred-foot serpent. And in 1894, a similar creature appeared to 70-year-old farmer Austin Rice much farther north in East Deerfield, Mass. The *Boston Herald* published an article about the encounter that was reprinted frequently in local papers throughout the year.

Could these sightings over eight years all have been the same creature or even the same species of creature? It certainly seems that way. In fact, encounters have occurred throughout New England. As far north as Vermont and as far south as Long Island Sound, stories have persisted about a serpent or family of serpents that live in the Connecticut River.

In modern times, those testing for their boat licenses near the mouth of the river are told to beware of "Connie," an affectionate name that some use for the serpent. There are even unsubstantiated rumors that the creature lives in the Park River Tunnel in Hartford. This small tributary of the

Connecticut River was "buried" under the city starting in the 1940s, though part of the river and tunnel are still accessible to kayakers, who describe it as quite eerie.

Observations

Sage, Stocking, and other onlookers in 1886 described the Connecticut River Serpent as having a black head the width of a flour barrel and eyes the size of plates. During its two appearances, the creature displayed a neck up to 15 feet long, leading onlookers to guess that its full body must stretch at least 100 feet. Of particular note was how fast the serpent swam toward Gildersleeve Island.

The description given by Austin Rice of Massachusetts bears multiple similarities to the sighting in Connecticut. Rice explained that the creature's body was as thick as a stovepipe, black, and with a white stripe around its mouth that extended down its underbelly. He further noted the speed at which the serpent moved.

Finally, Capt. Sherman of the *Coral* again used the flour barrel comparison and further added that the creature's head resembled that of an alligator. Since the serpent was so close to the surface of the water, Sherman and his mate also observed that it was about 100 feet long and moved at "quite a rapid gait."

The commonalities around these sightings all center on the Connecticut River Serpent's size, speed, and color. Given the dark, clouded quality of New England rivers, it's possible that these traits function as a natural defense mechanism that has allowed the creature to evade capture for so long.

Important Note

As several historians have noted, one of the most puzzling things about the story of Silas Sage and Col. Stocking is that

Sage, according to town records, appears to have died in 1835 — more than three decades before the serpent sighting. Curiouser and curiouser ...

The Connecticut River Serpent

Cryptid Category: Aquatic

Notes: We took a canoe into the Park River Tunnel, and while we saw plenty of graffiti, we did not find any evidence of river serpent nesting. However, the center of the tunnel is quite dark, so there's hope for future discoveries.

East Haddam

Moshup the Giant

Sleeping Giant State Park in Hamden (see page 110) isn't the only place in Connecticut to have been touched by an enormous cryptid. In fact, Devil's Hopyard State Park in East Haddam is also home to a giant from Native American lore: the colossal being known as Moshup.

For the Mohegan Tribe, Wampanoag Tribe, and others, Moshup is a nature hero who represents the "large and great beings" of the world. To maintain the balance of life, Moshup is married to Granny Squannit, leader of the little people, or Makiawisug (see page 217). When there is bad weather in the region, it is because Moshup and Granny Squannit are having an argument.

In ancient times, Moshup was known for many great deeds, including the planned construction of a bridge from Connecticut to Long Island or from Massachusetts to Martha's Vineyard, depending on the telling. While using boulders to set the foundation for the bridge, Moshup felt a crab bite his bare feet. "Hopping mad" and in tremendous pain, Moshup threw the rest of the boulders willy-nilly, which is how the islands off the coast of lower New England were formed and why Connecticut's soil is so rocky.

However, Moshup wasn't done with his display of indignation. As he came ashore, the giant tramped his feet

in anger, creating multiple geological depressions in New York, Massachusetts, and Connecticut. Moshup's footprints, particularly Moshup's Rock in Uncasville, Conn., are considered sacred sites by many Indigenous peoples.

In Connecticut, Moshup's footprints can also be found in Old Lyme and, of course, at Devil's Hopyard State Park. That being the case, it's reasonable to wonder why Devil's Hopyard isn't called "Moshup's Hopyard."

One theory about this unfortunate naming convention is that it was used by early European colonizers to denigrate native beliefs. Christian missionaries changed "Moshup" to "Satan" and warped Indigenous traditions to serve the missionaries' own purposes. Another example goes back to the source of bad weather: According to the missionaries, storms weren't caused by Moshup and Granny Squannit arguing, but rather by Satan in the form of Moshup whipping his wife in the form of Granny Squannit.

Given these unwarranted attacks on his character, it is little wonder that Moshup is thought by some to have left the area. Some coastal tribes believe that Moshup and his family transformed into whales and that rough seas in Long Island Sound and the North Atlantic are caused by Moshup's changing moods. Other people believe that Moshup still wanders the northeast.

Interestingly, Moshup counted another cryptid among his companions: a giant toad! Though it is located in Massachusetts on Martha's Vineyard, Moshup's Toad can be seen in the town of Aquinnah. According to the Wampanoag Tribe, Moshup turned his giant pet to stone before disappearing from New England.

Observations

No matter the tale or variation, Moshup is symbolic of the link between the land and the sea. He is a giant of tremendous strength and stature, able to lift massive rocks, build colossal structures, and wade safely in the depths of the Atlantic Ocean.

In some versions of Moshup's tale, he is so angry after getting bitten by the crab that his feet turn red hot. This is how Moshup was able to leave his footprints in solid rock throughout the region.

Both Moshup and Granny Squannit possess what non-Indigenous people might call nature "magic." Their moods affect the weather and the seas, and Moshup was able to encase his pet toad in solid rock.

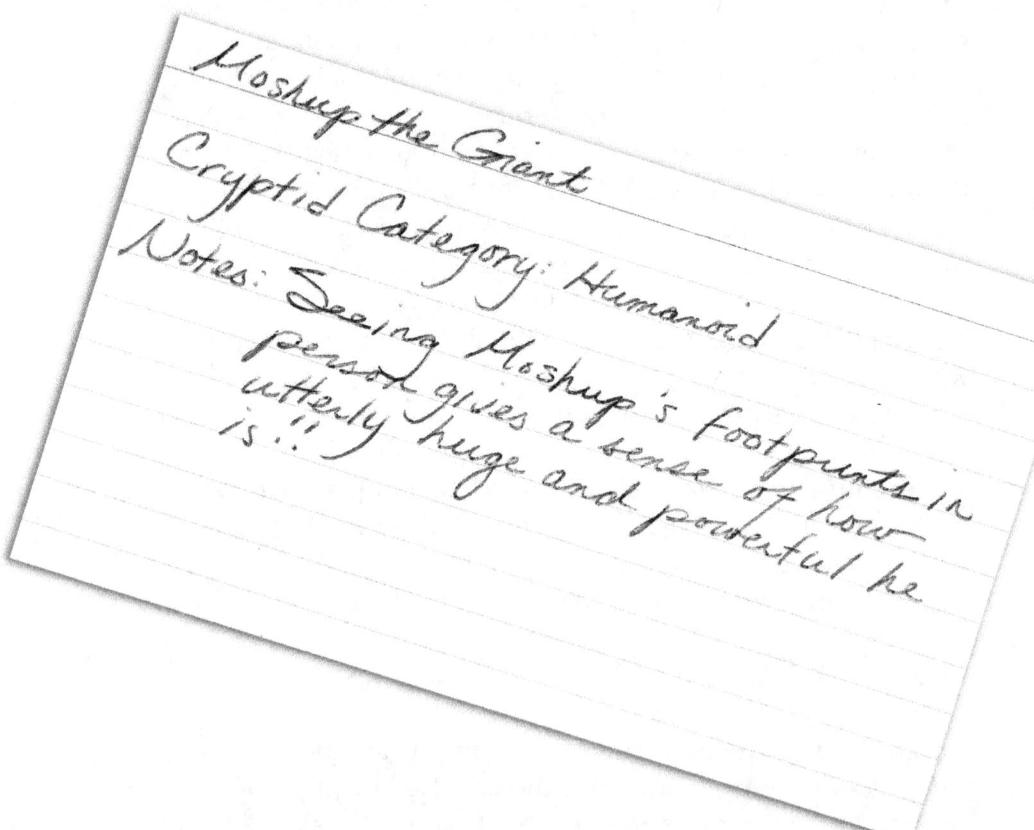

East Hampton & Others

Bigfoot's Visit to Connecticut

In the course of researching Connecticut's cryptid population, Val and I spoke to nearly every historical society in the state. When it came time to contact the Chatham Historical Society in East Hampton, the response we got to our inquiry was: "Well, we did have a Bigfoot sighting in 2004 or 2005."

This simple statement opened the door to investigating Bigfoot's presence in the Nutmeg State. Of course, East Hampton isn't the only spot where the famous Sasquatch has been sighted, but it is the place where we begin our journey.

If any cryptid has captured the public's collective imagination, it is certainly Bigfoot. Sightings are common in the Pacific Northwest and northern California, which is where the famous Patterson-Gimlin footage showing Bigfoot in his iconic "striding" pose was shot in 1967.

However, this doesn't mean that the West Coast has a monopoly on Bigfoot sightings. On the contrary, there is plenty of lore right here in Connecticut from as far back as the 1890s and as recently as 2019.

The East Hampton incident occurred around Thanksgiving 2004. Two witnesses were cleaning up dinner when something struck the side of their home with enough force to shake the walls. When the witnesses went to investigate, they noticed that one of their exterior motion lights was on and that a large shadow was moving back into the woods. One of the witnesses then felt as if they were being watched for hours after the incident.

When members of the Bigfoot Field Researchers Association (BFRO) conducted an investigation the following spring, they spoke to others in the area who had had similar encounters over the years.

In 2012, the Animal Planet television series *Finding Bigfoot* visited Connecticut to investigate other Sasquatch sightings. Though no towns are specifically named in the episode, members of BFRO travelled to greater Waterbury, the Northwest Hills, and the northeastern parts of the state. Among the people interviewed was Tonya DeAngelis, who lived in Ridgefield at the time and had captured possible Bigfoot footage while taking a cell phone video of her two children riding their bikes.

Another event occurred in 2018, when a U.S. Army serviceman was hiking in the People's State Forest in Barkhamsted and discovered giant 15-inch footprints. The man took a cast of the prints and provided them to BFRO.

These are just a handful of stories that circulate among Bigfoot enthusiasts in Connecticut. One hypothesis is that our heavily wooded state is a pass-through for Bigfoot creatures as they migrate north or west. Another theory is that New England and New York have their own distinct Bigfoot populations, to which some of the other creatures in this field guide are perhaps related.

Observations

Most Bigfoot sightings share a few commonalities: a hominid creature of significant stature with dark fur and a long stride. Some sightings include variations on the creature's size and the color of its pelt.

Sound, too, often plays a role in Bigfoot sightings. Some witnesses hear footsteps or loud bangs, as in the East

Y
UCONN
MAKE CT
WEIRD!

Hampton incident. Others hear "wood knocks," a noise that is like two pieces of wood being struck together. Still others hear otherworldly moans, cries, or screams.

One particularly notable sighting was reported in the June 29, 1898, issue of the *Naugatuck Daily News* in which four men from Danbury encountered the "Cotton Hollow Wild Man" in the state forest between Naugatuck and Beacon Falls. The four men were returning to their campsite just before midnight when "a man of gigantic stature sprang up in front of them from among the bushes and shouted out ... 'How far is it to the next town?'" Startled, the men from Danbury offered directions, whereupon the wild man (or creature) "started off on a wild run and disappeared in the woods and the dark."

The next day, the men from Danbury decided to investigate what had happened the night before. They found footprints nearby that were 18.5 inches long and 5.5 inches broad. After asking among local residents, the men learned that this "giant among giants" was a common sight in the area. He was reported to be at least nine feet tall and weigh 500 pounds. And apparently, this Bigfoot had also added human speech to his list of tricks.

Bigfoot in Connecticut

Cryptid Category: Humanoid

Notes: So many wonderful researchers have contributed to the pool of knowledge about Bigfoot's presence in CT. Our work continues, and I am confident that we are on the verge of a breakthrough!

Essex

The Glowackus, Successor to the Glawackus

n 1966, the national mood in America was grim. There were protests against the Vietnam War, escalating tensions with Cuba, and unrest as a result of the Civil Rights Movement. Given the steady stream of seemingly bad news, it is little surprise that Alfred "Fred" Knapp wanted to do something to bring a bit of levity to his community. Unfortunately, Knapp's prank involving a cryptid called the Glowackus backfired so spectacularly that it nearly ended in his arrest and the arrest of several others.

On Sept. 15 of that year, Knapp published an article in the local *New Era* newspaper about a strange encounter that had occurred during the "Essex Autumn Ride" four days prior. Seven horsemen led by Dr. Roy D. Kelley, a local optometrist, were riding near the Great Pequot Swamp when they saw what they initially thought was a bear. The creature had planted itself firmly in the middle of the trail and had begun making a strange noise. It was soon clear to all that this was no ordinary woodland beast.

Dr. Kelley charged the creature with his horse, causing the creature to flee back into the woods. The group quickly moved on, with Edmund O'Brien lingering behind to make sure the beast did not pursue the riders. Unfortunately for O'Brien, the creature reappeared from the brush to once

again utter its uncanny cry. In desperation, O'Brien used the flash on his camera to try and scare the monster away.

The tactic worked, and the creature fled for good. More importantly, though, was the fact that O'Brien had captured photographic proof of the monster's existence. This photo, featuring an inhuman face framed by vines and leaves, accompanied Knapp's story in *The New Era* newspaper. The article also included an interview with Essex First Selectman Escott MacWhinney, who claimed that the creature was the Glastonbury Glawackus. Unfortunately, Knapp misspelled the name as "Glowackus" and invented a new set of attributes for the creature drawn from the fictional encyclopedia *Mooseheim's Memorabilia of Monsters.*

In the hours and days after the story of the Glowackus was published, police received more than 60 phone calls from residents concerned that a monster was lurking in their midst. Adults and children alike were fearful of leaving their homes, so officers from both the Connecticut State Police and the Old Saybrook Police Department descended on Essex to both reassure residents and interview Knapp.

At this point, Knapp admitted that the whole thing had been a hoax perpetrated by him, Kelley, and MacWhinney. (There is no mention of O'Brien, though he was likely involved as well.) All three men were threatened with legal action, especially after police found the Glowackus mask during a search of Knapp's home. "The story upset the community to a considerable degree," State Police Lt. Joseph Hart told the *New Haven Register* two days later on Sept. 17.

On Sept. 22, *The New Era* published a retraction in which Knapp explained that the joke had been intended to take people's minds off of Vietnam and Cold War headlines. In addition to the five dozen police calls, The *New Era* had also fielded more than 200 phone calls from readers seeking clarification on the Glowackus story.

For their part, Knapp and MacWhinney were shocked that the tall tale had been taken so literally, resulting in a localized hysteria reminiscent of the 1938 *War of the Worlds* radio broadcast. Part of the blame surely fell on the shoulders of *The New Era,* since the newspaper presented the article as serious news, with no indication whatsoever that it was satire. Notably, future articles about the Glowackus included the subheads "Not To Be Taken Seriously" and "Strictly for Laughs."

Observations

Though Knapp was trying to draw on the story of the Glastonbury Glawackus for his fictional creation, the Essex Glowackus can be viewed as a unique cryptid with its own characteristics. Knapp's original article describes the Glowackus as being the size of a man and covered in brown, mink-like fur. It has a small, piggish face, two sets of ears, and a ruff at the base of its short neck. Each of its four paws is topped by curved talons.

Knapp drew on additional details from the nonexistent *Mooseheim's Memorabilia of Monsters*, which allegedly contained a lengthy entry on the Glowackus. First observed in 1900, the Glowackus has no tail and is able to walk upright or on all fours. It is carnivorous, and its fur emits a strange glow, from which the creature draws its name. Of particular note is the Glowackus' unique cry, which Knapp described as sounding like "wackus" or "ackus."

Compare these attributes with those of the fearsome Glawackus, and it's clear that Knapp and his accomplices successfully created a whole new cryptid — one just for their community of Essex.

Haddam

The Higganum Mucket

There must be something about bodies of water named "Candlewood" that is particularly attractive to Connecticut cryptids. Not only is Candlewood Lake in western Connecticut home to a fearsome aquatic creature (see page 6), but so too is Candlewood Hill Brook in the Higganum section of Haddam. For it is in these waters that the Higganum Mucket has its only spawning grounds on the entire planet.

Most of what we know about the Higganum Mucket comes from the exhaustive work of famed cryptozoologist Arthur Wiknik Jr., who has been studying the Mucket since the 1980s. It is through Wiknik's extensive writings that the Mucket came to be known outside of Higganum, where the creatures have been an important part of community lore for much, much longer.

The origins of the Mucket are murky at best. It's possible the species lived in other locations, like Argentina, and either died out or have remained so hidden as to yet be discovered by modern cryptid researchers. One theory is that the Mucket is of extraterrestrial origin and that the creatures were seeded in Connecticut as pets or food for future alien visitors. Why Candlewood Hill Brook was chosen is unclear, but Wiknik explains that the Muckets stay in the brook

because "the aliens left behind a galactic sphere that releases cosmic elements into the water to make the fish think they are on their home planet."

The Mucket herd lived relatively undisturbed in Candlewood Hill Brook until the 1800s, when several dams were built in the area to provide power for local mills. The creatures, though, quickly adapted. Muckets began using their powerful tailfins to leap upstream and over the dams. The sight of these rotund creatures flying through the air was said to rival that of yearly salmon migrations.

Unfortunately, Muckets did not fare quite as well during the infamous Connecticut Flood of 1982. This historic storm dumped 16 inches of water on parts of the state over four days and caused an estimated $230 million in damage. It also decimated the Mucket population.

This tragedy, as well as the destruction of the nearby Frismar factory in August 1989, led to the founding of the Mucket Recovery Program, which coincided with the adoption of the Mucket as a town mascot. Whereas Mucket hunts once took place regularly to ensure that the herd remained at a manageable size, the creatures now began to be revered as a kind of good-luck charm.

For example, new recruits to the Haddam Volunteer Fire Department are sometimes tasked with catching a Mucket as part of their initiation. In 2012, Haddam's 350th anniversary committee hosted a Mucket art contest for students at Haddam-Killingworth Middle School. And in 2020, the Haddam Economic Development Commission began planning for an annual "Mucket Madness Day," which was unfortunately delayed because of the COVID-19 global pandemic.

Today, the Mucket population is rebounding. Given how long the species has been around and its unparalleled adaptability, it's likely that this strange fish will continue to call Higganum home for a long time to come.

Observations

Adult Muckets can grow to 18 inches in length, though young specimens, known as "calves," are slightly smaller. A typical Mucket has a catfish-like body with sharp scales and a forked tail. Its head, though, is more like that of a lizard, with broad lips and razor teeth that are constantly sharpened by its rough tongue.

Male Muckets are known as "bulls" and sport two curved horns, about an inch in length, atop their lumpy skulls.

Some bulls grow a third horn on their lower jaw, which was a highly prized commodity prior to the launch of the Mucket Recovery Program.

Female Muckets are known as "cows." They do not have horns but instead have warty skin pigmentation that can act as a defense mechanism. When threatened, this pigmentation can assume a variety of forms, such as a third eye, to ward off predators. Even before the Mucket Recovery Program, it was illegal to hunt female Muckets.

All Muckets subsist on hellgrammite larva, an aquatic organism that is abundant in fresh water rivers. Muckets have also been known to catch squirrels or opossums that wander too close to Candlewood Hill Brook. Muckets will bite humans if threatened. A Mucket's bite is venomous, though suggestions that the creature's saliva can lead to baldness seem too fantastical to believe.

The Higganum Mucket

Cryptid Category: Semi - Aquatic

Notes: Had a fantastic call with Art Wiknik, who was kind enough to provide copies of his original reseach papers on the Mucket. He is truly one of Connecticut's greatest cryptozoologists!

Old Saybrook

The Blockheads

A popular stereotype is that people who claim to have seen UFOs are willing to stretch rationality. When someone with a tinfoil hat says they saw a flying saucer, society laughs it off. But when a respected, highly educated member of the community swears that extraterrestrial creatures exist, it becomes much harder to dismiss.

Mary M. Starr certainly fell into the second category. Born in Holyoke, Mass., in 1890, Starr attended college in Vermont and, after graduation, travelled to China and Japan. She returned to America in the 1920s, taught languages at East Hartford High School, and received a master's degree from Yale in 1930. She then jetted off to continue her studies in Europe, where she became friends with the exiled royal family of Greece. She even wrote an article about King George II of Greece for the *Hartford Courant*!

During World War II, Starr's knowledge of Japanese and Chinese languages landed her a consulting gig with the FBI. After the attack on Pearl Harbor in 1941, she and her son, Robin, opened their home in Essex to servicemen who were on leave or recuperating in the United States. Over a period of several years, Starr offered respite to more than 2,000 Allied sailors. For her work, she received public thanks from both the U.K. Parliament and the British Admiralty.

In late 1945, following Robin's death at the Battle of Okinawa, Starr sold her home in Essex and moved to Indiana, where she became a dean at Hobart High School. The death of her son had had a profound impact on her. In 1947, she told the *Courant* that her house, which had affectionately been known as the "HMS Connecticut" during the war, held too many memories of Robin.

Starr returned to Connecticut sometime in the 1950s and settled in Old Saybrook. It was here, in 1957, that she encountered something otherworldly. The event was so strange, in fact, that she didn't speak about it until nearly a year later, when she reported it to the National Investigations Committee on Aerial Phenomena (NICAP). A UFO group based out of New York then published the details of Starr's sighting in its July 1959 newsletter.

Sometime between 2 and 3 a.m. on Dec. 16, 1957, Starr was awoken by bright lights passing her bedroom window. This, in and of itself, was unusual because most of the cottages around hers were empty for the season. As she watched, a large vehicle about 10-20 feet long and with square portholes came to a stop between her house and the tool shed in her yard. At first, Starr thought it was a troop carrier that had gotten lost. She then realized that the vehicle was much more unusual than a typical troop transport. For one thing, it was floating about five feet off the ground.

As Starr watched, several individuals passed by the vehicle's backlit portholes. They made a few strange movements before the lights inside faded. An antenna rose, and the entire craft seemed to glow. After a few more moments, the vehicle reversed back the way it had come, "tilted steeply, and shot up into the sky at the speed of a jet take-off." The vehicle made no noise during its entire visit.

The report concludes that, "Because of her background, and because she had no conceivable reason to invent or embellish such a story, [Civilian Saucer Intelligence] places it in the authentic category."

The Old Saybrook Blockheads, as they came to be known, never visited the area again — or did they? Not much is known about Mary Starr's life between 1960, when she left Connecticut again to take up a new teaching post in Leesburg, Va., and 1982, when she died in Hartford one month shy of her 92nd birthday. In fact, state newspapers didn't even publish an obituary about her passing!

So, what was Starr doing during these 22 years? Is it possible the Blockheads returned and invited this extraordinary earthling to travel with them for a while? That would certainly explain the gap in the public record. For all we know, Mary Starr lived the final chapter of her life going where no one had gone before as she became humanity's first expert on alien languages.

Observations

Mary Starr's report offers a detailed description of the three individuals whom she saw inside the vehicle that landed near her cottage. The beings, she said, walked with their right arms raised and wore pale robes or jackets that flared at the bottom. They did not appear to have hands. Given the dimensions of the vehicle relative to Starr's clothesline and tool shed, she estimated that the craft was about four feet high, which meant that the Blockheads had to be shorter than four feet to fit inside their vehicle.

The most unusual characteristic of the beings, though, was their heads. Instead of having features like eyes, nose, ears, and mouth, Starr said that the creatures had square or rectangular heads that were reddish-orange in color with bright red bulbs in the center. This is where the Blockheads get their name, though Starr couldn't discount the possibility that they were wearing helmets. Before the light faded from the portholes, she could see nothing else inside the vehicle in terms of instrumentation or other features.

It is not known why the Blockheads visited Old Saybrook, though nothing about Starr's account suggests that the beings were malevolent. It is also reasonable to assume that the Blockheads have advanced technology based on the swift and silent operation of their vehicle.

Fun Fact

A collectible card game called MetaZoo: Cryptid Nation that launched in 2020 features a rare promo card based on the Old Saybrook Blockheads. The creators of the game clearly did their homework. Other Connecticut cryptids featured in MetaZoo include the Black Dog of the Hanging Hills and the Glastonbury Glawackus.

The Old Saybrook Blockheads

Cryptid Category: unknown

Notes: The life of Mary Starr is so interesting, her encounter with the Blockheads notwithstanding. It truly took a village to research the life of this important figure in CT cryptozoological history.

Northeastern Connecticut

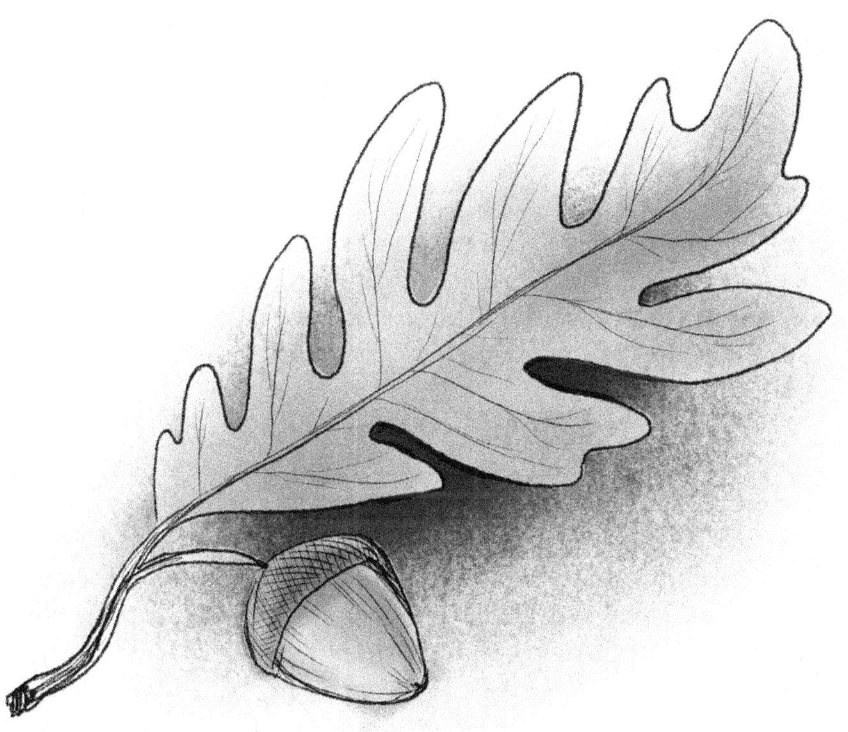

Windham

The Battle of the Frogs

The clock had just struck midnight one evening in June 1754 when groans began to fill the air. In the pitch darkness, the bellows seemed to come from everywhere at once and, at times, even sounded like they were forming incoherent words.

Shocked and alarmed, the residents of Windham bolted upright in their beds. Was someone in trouble? Was the village under attack? Or had Judgment Day finally come to claim their souls? It was only after dawn broke that Windhamites would venture forth from their homes to learn the awful truth.

To be sure, the 1750s were a stressful time for Connecticut and the Thirteen Colonies as a whole. Rumors of conflict were growing as the French and Indian War got underway. Benjamin Franklin published his famous "Join or Die" illustration, which would become an enduring icon of the American Revolution two decades later. And religious fervor was at an all-time high thanks to the effects of the so-called Great Awakening 10 years prior.

Into this climate stepped the 1,000 or so residents of Windham. Located about 30 miles east of Hartford, Windham was considered for many years to be "the most important town in that section of the State." Comprised mostly of farms and mills, the community took advantage of local rivers

to power its way of life. Indeed, it was one of these very waterways that caused all the trouble that summer in 1754.

According to various accounts — some true, some exaggerated — the noise came on suddenly and built to a cacophony. Many villagers prayed for salvation, while others organized a party of armed men to investigate the disturbance and keep watch. As the sun rose, the source of the commotion became clear: Something had killed dozens, and perhaps hundreds, of bullfrogs at a nearby pond.

But what had caused this calamitous event? To this day, it's not clear. Some unverified reports claim that Connecticut was in the midst of a drought that summer and that the frogs had fought to the death over a steadily shrinking pond. A more plausible explanation is that the frogs were making "advertisement calls" as part of their breeding behavior. With too many males and a shrinking habitat — whether from drought or human settlement — the frogs were competing for mates by calling over one another ... loudly!

Whatever the reason, the event soon became enshrined in legend. The pond where the "frog battle" occurred became forever known as Frog Pond, and a plaque was placed at the site (though it was later moved to the town green). Poems, ballads, songs, and even an operetta were written about the event, with varying levels of hyperbole.

Rather than shy away from the tale, Windham has embraced its reputation as the "village of bullfrogs." Notes issued by the old Windham Bank in the 1800s were appropriately called "greenbacks" and featured a pair of bullfrogs. The town seal and logo also include frogs.

But most impressive of all is the Thread City Crossing, affectionately known as the "Frog Bridge." Built in 2000 and spanning the Willimantic River, the Thread City Crossing features four giant frog sculptures crouched atop four giant spools of thread (the spools pay homage to Willimantic's historic textile industry). The frogs — two at each end of the bridge — even have names: Willy, Manny, Windy, and Swifty.

Though the Battle of the Frogs occurred nearly three centuries ago, it's clear that these amphibians have had a profound impact on Windham's history. With the Thread City Crossing now an offbeat tourist destination, it's expected that these leaping cryptids will continue to exert an influence on the area for many years to come.

Observations

American Bullfrogs can be found all over North America, generally residing in freshwater lakes, ponds, bogs, and slow-moving streams. Frog Pond, with Indian Hollow Brook at its north and sound ends, is obviously an ideal habitat for these creatures, then and now.

According to Connecticut's Beardsley Zoo, bullfrogs are

the largest frog species in North America. They're about six to six-and-a-half inches long and weigh two ounces. Their skin varies in tone from bright to dull green, and they have incredibly strong hind legs. Males are larger than females.

What sets bullfrogs apart from their counterparts is their call, which sounds like a horn or bellows. A bullfrog will expand its body to nearly the bursting point before trumpeting out. Multiplied by the dozens, one can imagine what kind of racket this made in 1754.

The Beardsley Zoo further notes that bullfrogs are "known for their voracious appetite and aggressive behavior, even as tadpoles." Therefore, it's not difficult to imagine how this could have led to the Battle of the Frogs that fateful night in the mid-eighteenth century.

Important Note

Some early sources, like Brigham Payne's *The Story of Bacchus and Centennial Souvenir*, erroneously give the date of the Battle of the Frogs as 1758. The more accepted year, as confirmed by the Windham Historical Society, is 1754.

The Battle of the Frogs

Cryptid Category: Semi-Aquatic

Notes: Val and I visited a vernal pool during mating season for the Spring Peeper to get a sense of what the "Frog Fight" might have sounded like. If this one, small pool is any indication, the Windham frogs would have made quite a racket!

Woodstock

The White Deer

Due in part to superstitions and in part to rarity, there has long been a debate among individuals who hunt game for sport and sustenance whether it is ethical to kill animals with albinism (an overall absence of pigment) and leucism (a partial absence of pigment that results in a piebald appearance). Some U.S. states — but not all — have laws that prohibit the hunting of such animals. This means that hunting communities often have to police themselves, either privately or, in the internet age, in the court of public opinion. Even then, beliefs are split between those who view animals with albinism and leucism as special and those who see them as legitimate game.

Surely, this folktale from Woodstock falls into the former category — and serves as a cautionary tale.

The years 1885 and 1886 were said to be difficult ones for those who worked the land. The summer of '85 was cold, wet, and short, leading to poor crop yields. Winter came early and with a vengeance. Frost wiped out late-season produce, and the skies dumped foot after foot of snow on the region. By January '86, food was scarce and people were hungry.

One farmer, Jacob Smidly, was desperate to feed his family. On Jan. 15, 1886, Jacob loaded his rifle, leashed his

hound, and set out into the snowy woods with his son. They hoped to score some small game to tide them over.

Deep snow made the going difficult. After two hours trudging through the drifts, everyone was tired. That was when Jacob spotted a target greater than any he could have hoped for: a full-grown white deer. This was no squirrel or rabbit — a deer would feed his family for weeks!

As Jacob sighted along his rifle, both he and his son noticed how unusual this particular deer truly was. Its coat was completely white and its eyes were pink. Strangest of all was the fact that it had only one horn.

Jacob's son begged his father not to shoot the deer, but the family was in dire need of food. A shot rang out, and the unusual creature dropped to the snowpack.

Jacob began gutting the deer before dragging the corpse back to the family farm. Once home, he cut and stored the meat while tossing everything that wasn't edible into a rendering pit. His wife would be able to use the resulting fat for cooking or to make soap. Jacob also saved the deer's head, which he wanted as a trophy.

That night, Jacob brought the first of the venison inside for dinner. His son, though, refused to eat and ran outside with an upset stomach. The boy returned a moment later shouting that he had seen a red glow inside the shed where the rendering pit was located.

Worried that the shed had caught fire, Jacob ran outside. He did not come back. After a while, Jacob's worried wife and son ventured out to the shed to investigate. What they found was shocking. Jacob was dead in the rendering pit with blood on his shirt and a hole through his chest. All the meat he had stored from the white deer was gone, as well as all the fat from the rendering pit. The deer's head, too, was missing. All around the shed were hoof prints, as if a whole herd of deer had stampeded past. But that was surely impossible, since Jacob's wife and son would certainly have seen or heard such a large multitude of animals.

Jacob's death remained unexplained. The most common theory was that someone just as desperate and hungry had killed Jacob for the meat he had caught earlier that day. Unfortunately, that didn't explain the red glow, the lack of human footprints leading to and from the shed, or the method by which someone had gathered so much meat — to say nothing of the deer fat and deer head — in such a short amount of time.

Not long after, rumors began to spread among local residents about a white deer that roamed the forests of Woodstock. Notably, most hunters who stalked the area declined to fire upon this strange and elusive prey.

Observations

The story of Jacob Smidly is likely just that: a story. But the creature it portrays is undoubtedly real. Deer with albinism and leucism are rare. Reliable numbers are difficult to come by, but estimates range from 0.005 to 2 percent of the population.

For this reason, there is fierce debate in hunting circles about the ethics of killing animals with albinism and leucism in places where they are not protected by law. People who post about their kills online are often subject to public shaming and even death threats. There are also superstitions among hunters that those who kill animals with albinism or leucism will be dogged by misfortune for the rest of their days.

On the other side of the equation is the fact that these traits are recessive genetic abnormalities that often lead to other serious health problems such as birth defects, deformities, blindness, and disease. Notably, the story of Jacob Smidly claims that the white deer in Woodstock had only one horn. This seems to have some basis in scientific fact, since bucks with albinism often have stunted antlers. To keep these undesirable traits in check — no matter how rare — there is a biological argument to be made for hunting these animals.

No matter which side of the debate you fall on, animals with albinism and leucism can be found in Connecticut. Those who see them in the wild often cherish the experience as something special and even borderline spiritual.

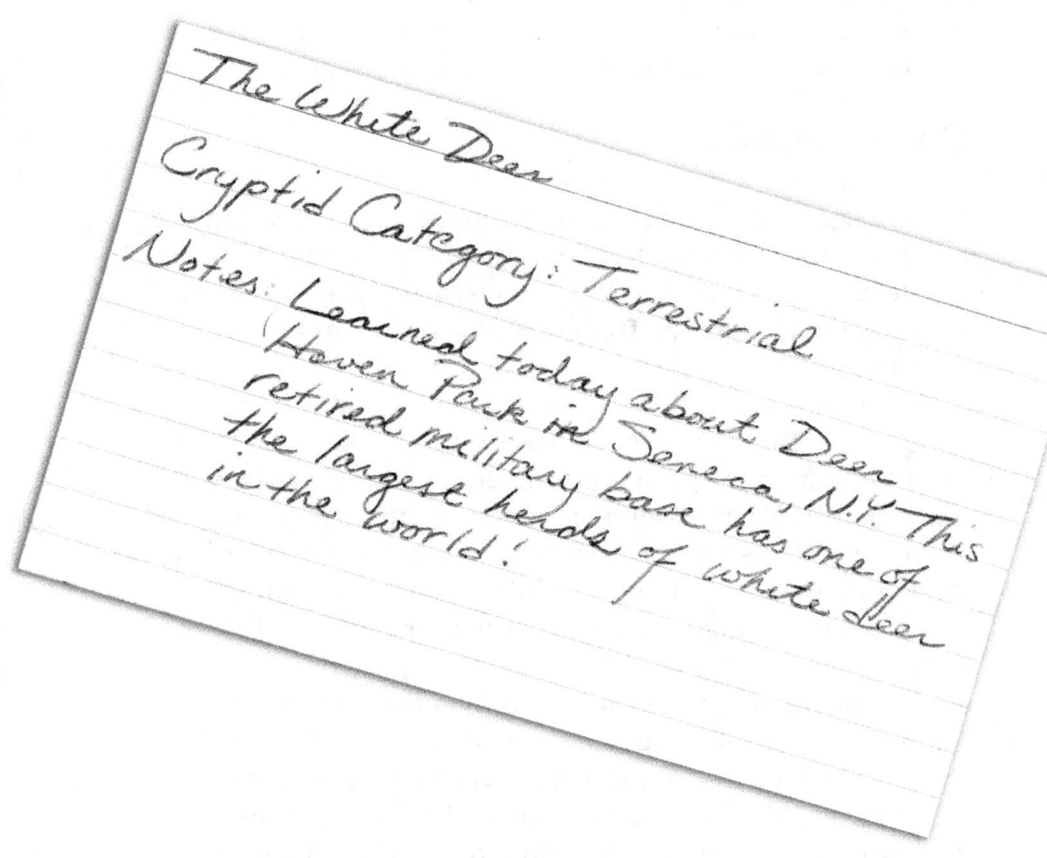

Southeastern
Connecticut

Franklin

The Worrineagues

One cold morning sometime prior to the 1890s, two men named Zeke and Peleg were preparing to bring a load of wool from the Pleasure Hill area of Franklin to a market in Norwich. The trip was approximately 15 miles, so they had gotten up in the predawn hours, loaded their cart, and yoked their oxen. It was just after 3 a.m. when they began driving through what is now Ayers Gap Preserve.

As they neared one of the preserve's many impressive rock formations, the oxen began to spook. Zeke, too, heard something in the air. He asked his partner if he had heard it as well.

"Yes," Peleg said, and he was terrified. The two men had tempted fate by leaving so early in the morning, and Peleg knew what was making noise up on the nearby rock shelf.

Not wanting to risk their lives or the lives of their oxen, Zeke and Peleg returned home. They would depart again for Norwich in a few hours, safe in the knowledge that they would not again encounter the Worrineagues of Worrineague Rock in the blessed light of day.

This is just one tale about the Worrineagues, creatures who have appeared in New England lore since the seventeenth century and whose name is spelled several different ways. Although Worrineagues have been spotted

in Wethersfield and even as far north as Hadley, Mass., their permanent den is located in Franklin, where they have cavorted in the dark for hundreds of years.

Let's start back in 1683 at the Boston witch trial of Mary Webster. Mary and her much older husband lived in poverty in Hadley, where she was much disliked by her neighbors. Disgusted by Mary's temper, "which was not the most placid," locals accused her of witchcraft and sent her packing to the Court of Assistants in Boston.

During Mary's indictment, one of the accusations against her was that she had had relations with the devil "in the shape of a warraneage." Historians generally take "warraneage" to mean a fisher cat. This description, though, differs wildly from how Worrineagues are described by the time their stories reach Connecticut.

In a series of *Hartford Courant* articles from 1894, the Worrineagues take on an aspect that is more like dwarves or hobgoblins, and their actions become much more malicious. A letter to the editor from Oct. 3 of that year states that one of these creatures had been suspected of visiting Wethersfield five decades prior. The "wollaneag" or "woollynig" had the rough shape of a human but could breathe fire, walk on water, and emit a phosphorescent light. It also had horns and could not be harmed by bullets. The letter writer went on to state that the wollaneag was eventually revealed to be a man who had taken fantastical measures to frighten trespassers off his property.

The Worrineagues' description changes again when we get to the main legends in Franklin. Instead of cats or fire-breathing hominids, the Worrineagues are portrayed as small, barrel-bodied creatures who dance at night on Worrineague Rock while trying to tempt unwary travelers. And although there are plenty of warnings about avoiding the Worrineagues, there is scant information on what will happen if they actually get their hands on you.

Observations

The Worrineagues make their home exclusively at Worrineague Rock, where their nightly revels are accompanied by hollering noises. Their small bodies have short necks, hands without arms, and feet capable of dancing with "frightful facility." They are even able to turn themselves invisible.

It is not known where the name Worrineague comes from, though some historians suggest that the term originated from an Algonquian word. Likewise, it is not known how many Worrineagues reside at the main settlement in Franklin or if these creatures are related to any of the other species of little people that call Connecticut home.

Fun Fact

An interesting sidenote to the Mary Webster story is that she was exonerated by the court but her neighbors tried to hang her anyway. Miraculously, she survived the ordeal and lived until 1696. While it's not known if any Worrineagues helped her escape the noose, we do know that one of Webster's descendants is the author Margaret Atwood. Atwood wrote a poem about Mary and dedicated the famous novel *The Handmaid's Tale* to her.

The Worrineagues

Cryptid Category: Terrestrial

Notes: Why do the Worrineagues dance at night? Is it some kind of mating ritual? Do they have a kind of intelligence that eludes us?

Franklin

The Horse Creature

Jim **Wheeler was just about** to enter his teens in the mid-1990s when he crossed paths with an uncanny creature that he said will be burned into his memory until the day he dies. In an area called Whippoorwill Hollow, slightly southwest of Ayer's Gap Preserve, he met the "horse creature." That's the best description one can give to this equine terror, which remains distressingly unclassified by cryptozoologists.

As a young man, Jim and his twin brother worked at a small local farm where their responsibilities included the care of animals. The brothers helped feed the pigs and sheep, while also doing other odd jobs around the farm property.

One day, the brothers were dismayed to discover that the pigs had gotten out of their pen. The two split up in pursuit of the escaped hogs, searching first the farm property and then the surrounding woods. Jim hadn't gone far when he realized that he wasn't alone. Rearing up among the trees, its coat the color of snow, was a creature that partly resembled a horse.

As Jim watched, the beast bucked wildly up and down, almost in a running motion. However, the creature never

seemed to move any closer, nor did it make any noise. Even stranger was the fact that the creature didn't seem to have the long body of a horse; Jim instead described it as looking at the front of a horse head-on..

Not waiting to see if the creature would charge him, Jim ran back to the farm to retrieve his brother, whom he described as "much braver than I was." Unfortunately, the creature was gone by the time they returned to the scene of the sighting. Jim also told the farm owners about the creature, expecting to be laughed at for having an overactive imagination. Instead, the farm owners weren't particularly surprised to hear that Jim had seen something unusual in the woods.

Observations

To this day, Jim Wheeler insists that what he saw wasn't a horse. For one thing, the farm that he worked at didn't keep horses, and the nearest farm that did was several miles away. For another, Jim was well acquainted with what horses looked like. This, he said, was larger and moved in an erratic way that was disturbing.

So, what was it?

One theory is that Jim encountered some kind of water horse. These creatures go by many names — kelpie, *ceffyl dwfr, cabyll-ushtey, each uisce*, etc. — and feature in folklore from around the world, especially Celtic traditions. Though the stories vary wildly, one common element is the water horse's ability to change shape. This may explain why the horse creature only looked like a horse when stared at from straight ahead.

Water horses are almost universally malignant. Some live in the sea or in large bodies of still water, while others live in fast-running lakes and streams. This is notable since Whippoorwill Hollow Road borders Gagers Pond and Beaver Brook at the road's north end.

Furthermore, water horses can appear in many guises to lure their victims. The end goal is often to drown and eat unwary individuals who approach the water horse or, worse, try to ride on its back.

In other words, it's fortunate that Jim didn't hang around long enough to be snagged by the horse creature that day long ago. Otherwise, he likely wouldn't be here to tell us about it today.

The Horse Creature

Cryptid Category: Fae

Notes: Val and I have never been so terrified and disturbed by something in our lives.

Griswold

The Jewett City Vampires

Unless you're reading the latest Stephen King thriller, New England isn't usually considered a hotbed of vampire activity. Sure, King "staked" his claim on 'Salem's Lot in Maine, but Americans are more likely to turn to the South for their vampire fix, thanks to Anne Rice's Vampire Chronicles and Charlaine Harris' Sookie Stackhouse series (i.e. HBO's *True Blood*).

Maybe that shouldn't be the case though. Just as Connecticut played a lesser-known role in the witchcraft hysteria of the late-seventeenth century (see page 105), so too was the Nutmeg State caught up in the so-called Great New England Vampire Panic of the 1700s and 1800s. In fact, one of the most important archeological epicenters of this era is located in Griswold.

In 1990, children playing near a construction site in Griswold reported to their parents that they had found human bones. Originally, authorities were concerned that the remains were tied to a serial killer, until it became clear that the bones were actually quite old. At that point, then-State Archeologist Dr. Nicholas Bellantoni was called in to help with the investigation.

As sometimes happens, the construction in Griswold had revealed an unmarked burial site. These are fairly common in Connecticut and, indeed, most of New England.

In Griswold, the findings were typical of burials from 200 years prior — until they suddenly weren't. In a fieldstone crypt, in a red coffin with the initials "J.B." spelled out in brass tacks, came a startling discovery. The coffin had been smashed open, the skeleton beheaded, and the ribs fractured. Moreover, J.B.'s thigh bones had been arranged on top of his chest in a skull-and-crossbones motif.

What had happened here?

As Bellantoni continued his investigation, he began consulting with folklorist and researcher Michael E. Bell of Rhode Island. Bell's specialty was — and continues to be — vampirism in America. He and other colleagues pointed Bellantoni to the story of the Jewett City Vampires.

In 1845, in the Jewett City section of Griswold, a man named Lemuel B. Ray died at age 24. Four years later, Lemuel's father, Henry B. Ray, reportedly died of tuberculosis. And two years after that, Lemuel's brother, Elisha H. Ray, died at age 26.

Clearly, something troubling was happening to the Ray family. When the next oldest son, Henry Nelson Ray, contracted tuberculosis in 1854, the rest of the family decided that drastic action was needed.

On May 8, 1854, members of the Ray family and the community at large tramped down to the Jewett City Cemetery to conduct a purifying ritual. Convinced that Lemuel and Elisha had been turned into vampires and were now draining the life force of the living, the mob exhumed the bodies of the two brothers and "burned them on the spot," according to the *Norwich Weekly Courier.* Why Henry B. Ray was not exhumed remains a mystery.

Unfortunately, the plan did not succeed. A restored gravestone in another part of the cemetery shows that Henry Nelson Ray died later in 1854. Town records indicate that his wife and children also died of tuberculosis shortly thereafter.

If the undead Ray brothers weren't causing a tuberculosis outbreak with their nightly feedings, then who was? And how did this "vampire outbreak" begin in the first place? These

JB
55

questions lead us back to the grave of J.B. discovered in 1990.

Bellantoni's work, combined with local archival data, revealed that the unmarked burial ground at which J.B. was found was used until about 1830. Further forensic medical research showed that J.B. had likely died of tuberculosis. However, his tomb wasn't disturbed until about a decade after his death, or approximately 1840. This is just a few years before other members of the community — including the Ray family — started falling ill.

With this rough timeline, it's possible to hypothesize that J.B. was the progenitor vampire that started it all. J.B.'s grave is also, in the words of *Smithsonian Magazine*, one of the only intact vampire graves to have been found in the region, giving archeological credence to a theory that was once thought to be only myth.

Most interesting of all is that J.B. continues to be the subject of scientific inquiry. In 2019, researchers announced a likely identity for Griswold's resident vampire. Through a combination of DNA testing and local records, J.B. is thought to be a local farmer named John Barber.

Three years later, in 2022, forensic scientists used facial reconstruction software to give the world its first glimpse of what J.B. might have looked like. And so, after nearly 200 years, J.B. had both a name and a face to go with his enigmatic initials.

Observations

We don't know how much the Jewett City vampires resemble the bloodsuckers of popular media, but we do know that those bitten by this breed of vampire exhibit the symptoms of tuberculosis, also known as consumption. A wasting illness of the lungs, tuberculosis was prevalent — and deadly — for centuries before drug treatments for the disease were finally developed in the 1940s. Outbreaks were routinely blamed on vampires, with exhumations or purifying rituals performed in an attempt to stop these creatures' predations.

Vampires are often long lived or immortal, depending on the tradition to which one ascribes. Stealing the blood of others is how this longevity is achieved.

Knowing that, it is difficult to say if any vampires are still lurking in Connecticut today. In addition to the disturbed graves in Griswold, a disinterment also allegedly took place in Stafford when five out of six sisters there died of tuberculosis in the late 1800s.

As such, those who decide to go in search of these predators today would do well to keep their talismans close at hand in case any decide to awaken — and are hungry.

Important Note

The Jewett City Cemetery is open to the public during daytime hours and is located at the end of Anthony Street in Griswold. If you're facing the front of the cemetery, the row of headstones for most of the Ray family is located in the center-right section, about midway back near the right walkway. Henry Nelson Ray's headstone is located in a newer part of the cemetery, just inside the main gate. The Jewett City Cemetery is also where the 1854 bonfire was held, though there is no evidence of it today.

Jewett City Vampires

Cryptid Category: Humanoid

Notes: I feel so disoriented. Am I bleeding? What is happ

Mystic

The Pigman

ocated between the towns of Groton and Stonington, Mystic is not actually its own municipality. However, you wouldn't know it given the area's overall popularity. As home to both Mystic Seaport and Mystic Aquarium — not to mention fine dining, a bustling downtown, and a quaint shopping village — Mystic is consistently ranked among the top tourist destinations in Connecticut.

Part of this appeal no doubt comes from Mystic's long history. Native Americans lived in the area for thousands of years before European colonizers arrived in the early 1600s. Within the next century, Mystic had grown to become one of Connecticut's major seaports.

With the passing of years has also come the accumulation of legends. Mystic is no stranger to ghost tales and seafaring folklore, so it would stand to reason that cryptids might also gravitate here. However, Mystic's local cryptid isn't some strange aquatic being, but instead a murderous land-based creature.

In the late 1970s, several high school boys were cavorting on the southern end of Holmes Street one evening when they heard a woman screaming. They followed the cries down to the waterfront near Mystic Drawbridge only to be confronted by a horrific sight: In the dim light, they saw what they first took to be a large man holding a woman beneath the surface

of the water. The boys shouted for the man to stop, but he continued his assault until the woman stopped moving and her body disappeared into the river.

Just as the boys were about to flee and call the police, the man turned toward them. It wasn't a man at all, but a bipedal creature with the face of a pig. The beast snorted and made other pig-like noises before it too dove into the water and disappeared. Neither the Pigman nor its unfortunate prey was seen again.

The boys reported the incident to police, but no trace of the creature or its victim was ever found. A local woman was allegedly reported missing around the same time, but her name and the status of her case have been lost in the decades since.

Of particular note is that the Mystic Pigman's appearance was preceded by sightings of a similar creature in Northfield, Vt. In 1971, several high school students encountered a human-like creature with white hair and cloven feet outside of a school dance. Around the same time, multiple pets in the area had gone missing and a local man even claimed to have stumbled upon the Pigman's lair hidden deep in the woods.

It is not known if the Northfield Pigman and the Mystic Pigman is the same creature. Given how close humans came to its den in Vermont, it's possible the Pigman fled south to escape further notice. Where it went after its deadly stop in Mystic is anyone's guess.

Observations

Descriptions of the Mystic Pigman claim that it is roughly the size of a man with a pig-like face capable of making swine vocalizations. It is not known if the Pigman is able to speak. Obviously the creature is able to swim, since it jumped into the Mystic River to escape from onlookers.

The Northfield Pigman, on the other hand, is estimated to be between five and six feet tall with beady eyes and a pig's snout. It is covered in fine, white hair and makes a screeching noise in the woods. Based on evidence found at its alleged den, the creature subsisted on small animals like pets and woodland creatures.

Whether they are the same or different, the Pigman creatures will attack humans if given the chance. In addition to the female victim in Mystic, a teenage boy was also supposedly kidnapped from a farm in Northfield.

The Mystic Pigman

Cryptid Category: Humanoid

Notes: Given what we know about the Pigman's past deeds, the idea of searching the woods for its den was frightening. We went well armed with bear (pig?) spray and noisemakers.

Uncasville

The Makiawisug

In **Mohegan culture,** as in many Native American traditions, balance is essential: dark and light, summer and winter, the natural world and the spirit world. Is it any wonder, then, that the giant beings of Mohegan belief are linked to the Little People, or Makiawisug, via the union of Moshup and Granny Squannit, respectively? Whereas Moshup represents the great beings of the world (and was responsible for some truly awe-inspiring deeds — see page 167), the Makiawisug (pronounced mah-key-ah-wee-sug) are aligned with the down-to-earth disciplines of agriculture and the healing arts.

From their home under Mohegan Hill in Uncasville, the Makiawisug have had a relationship with the Mohegan Tribe going back countless years. The Makiawisug taught the Mohegan people how to grow corn and how to use native plants for healing. In exchange, the Mohegans leave offerings for the Makiawisug and follow certain rules of etiquette in their presence.

For example, one should not look directly at the Makiawisug, since they find this rude. If the Makiawisug see you watching them, "they might point a finger at you, rooting you to the ground, while they take your belongings." Another variation of this finger-pointing power is that onlookers lose the ability to see the Makiawisug, allowing the Little People to take from you what they wish. One should also avoid speaking about the Makiawisug in summer, when they are most active. If they overhear you, they might become offended that you're talking about them.

Offerings to the Makiawisug are often left in small splint baskets made from either oak or ash. In particular, the Little People are fond of corn cakes, berries, tobacco, and, occasionally, meat. They will sometimes even come to a person's home looking for a meal, in which case it is prudent to give them whatever they ask.

After European colonists arrived in Connecticut, the Mohegan people entered a "time of Bad Spirits" in which many tribal members and their Makiawisug neighbors became ill. Animals and plants were fewer in number, and the Mohegans forgot to leave offerings for the Little People. Disease and hunger were widespread.

One evening, a Makiawisug named Weegun braved a ferocious storm to seek out the Mohegan medicine woman Martha Uncas. Weegun told Martha that one of the Makiawisug was gravely ill. Despite the weather, Martha gathered her things and followed Weegun out into the storm.

Weegun led Martha underground into a passage whose walls were painted with images from ancient stories. She then followed Weegun into the heart of the Makiawisug realm and finally into a "beehive-shaped chamber" where her patient was waiting. Martha was shocked to discover that it was none other than Granny Squannit who needed help.

Weegun and a girl named Ponemah explained that Granny Squannit was very sick and must be made well again. Martha didn't need to be told twice. After all, the Mohegan people looked to Granny Squannit when they themselves were in dire need of healing.

Martha ministered to Granny Squannit for nearly a month until the leader of the Makiawisug was well enough to leave bed. In return for Martha's service, Ponemah gave Martha a basket of gifts that included quartz crystals, painted skins,

herbs, and a black velvet belt woven with glass beads. The Little People then blindfolded Martha and led her home.

Martha, who lived until 1859, wasn't the only person to have seen and had a relationship with the Makiawisug. In addition to Martha's descendants, several Mohegan leaders were also said to interact with the Little People. Chief Matahga (Burrill Fielding) supposedly left baskets for the Makiawisug in the 1940s, while Chief Little Hatchet (Courtland Fowler) was said to have seen the Little People near the Tantaquidgeon Museum in 1984.

More recently, in 2012, the Mohegan Tribe blocked the creation of a housing development near Mohegan Hill because the construction had the potential to disturb sacred stone piles that had been created by the Makiawisug.

In a letter to the U.S. Department of Housing and Urban Development, Tribal Historic Preservation Officer James Quinn wrote, "These stone piles also possess powers that protect the Mohegan people from outsiders. Not only do the Little People still live within the ground on the Hill and continue to guard the stones, these stone piles are perceived as being made of the bones of Mother Earth and they contain messages that guide generation after generation of Mohegan people. Contemporary Mohegan tribal members make offerings to the Little People in hopes that they will continue to protect our Tribe."

In the end, the State Historic Preservation Office agreed. As of this writing, the land has not been developed and the Makiawisug have not been disturbed.

Observations

Because of their magic powers, one must be very surreptitious and respectful when observing the Makiawisug. Their arrival in an area is often heralded by the call of the whip-poor-will, a distinct song of one syllable, pause, and three rising syllables. This is also how Martha Uncas knew that Weegun had come to her home.

Another defining characteristic of the Makiawisug is their footwear. The Little People wear moccasin flowers for shoes, especially at night when they gather their offerings. In fact, the word "Makiawisug" is a combination of the Mohegan terms for "whip-poor-will" and "moccasins."

Like the Old Men of the Mountains in Canaan (see page 46), the Makiawisug are said to be the size of human children. Some accounts say that they are about knee-high, stout, and born from the earth.

The Makiawisug are also quite wise. Their teachings guide the Mohegan Tribe, particularly those who serve as culture-keepers and medicine folk. In addition, the Little People keep the earth healthy and will sometimes grant favors if asked. When bad weather descends on the area, it is because Granny Squannit and her husband, the giant Moshup, are arguing. Granny Squannit's severe illness during Martha Uncas' lifetime also caused a storm of considerable strength.

Lastly, the Makiawisug are masters of the healing arts. Tied to their knowledge of the earth and growing things, the Makiawisug are familiar with many kinds of medicinal plants and techniques. This is just one of the many things they taught the Mohegan Tribe.

Fun Fact

Born in 1761, Martha Uncas became a renowned culture-keeper for the Mohegan Tribe. Her descendants include many other notable culture-keepers, several of whom were said to have had personal contact with the Makiawisug. Among these was Martha's granddaughter, Fidelia "Flying Bird" Fielding (1827-1908), and Dr. Gladys Tantaquidgeon (1899-2005), both of whom inherited the black velvet belt that Martha received from Ponemah and Granny Squannit.

In particular, Gladys Tantaquidgeon lived an extraordinary life during her 106 years. She studied under anthropologist Frank Speck at the University of Pennsylvania and made tremendous strides to preserve Mohegan culture through her work as a medicine woman. In addition, she worked for the U.S. Bureau of Indian Affairs, fought for civil rights, and was instrumental in securing federal recognition for the Mohegan Tribe in 1994. She founded the Tantaquidgeon Museum in 1931, which is the oldest Native American-owned and operated museum in the United States. Her great-niece, Melissa Tantaquidgeon Zobel, carries on these traditions today as a Mohegan medicine woman and tribal historian.

The Makiawisug

Cryptid Category: Humanoid

Notes: Observing the Makiawisug is difficult because it is rude to stare at them. Insted, we made the proper offerings with a well-stocked Makiawisug basket, hoping for an invitation to talk.

BUT WHAT ABOUT...?

In the course of researching this book, Val and I came across many fascinating, weird, and creepy tales that neither of us had heard before — despite living in Connecticut our entire lives! The Nutmeg State has no shortage of ghost stories, which we were reminded of often when we spoke to historical society researchers, librarians, and members of the general public. And while ghosts and cryptids are both associated with the paranormal, most ghost stories were outside the scope of this book.

So, what to do with the stories that were close but didn't quite fit into the cryptid category? Or the ones that never panned out for lack of sources? Perhaps you've already leafed through the table of contents looking for your favorite tale, only to find that it isn't listed.

Before you fire off an angry email demanding an explanation for a particular omission, here are the stories that Val and I chose to leave out and the reasons why.

The Leather Man

I can't recall how many times Val and I spoke to people about cryptids, only to be asked, "Have you heard about the Leatherman?" After a while it became a bit of a joke during the production of this book.

So why is the Leatherman not included? Because he was a very real person with a very fascinating legacy!

In short, the Leatherman was a famous (human) vagabond whose regular circuit took him through parts of Connecticut and New York. If you'd like to learn more about him, check out *The Old Leather Man: Historical Accounts of a Connecticut and New York Legend* (Wesleyan University Press, 2008) by Dan W. DeLuca.

Problematic Tales

The Melonheads *(various towns):* This is the one that Val and I get asked about the most: Why didn't we include the Melonheads? The reasons are two-fold. First, the Melonheads are human (or formerly human) in most versions of the tale. Second, the story of the Melonheads is insensitive at best and exploitative at worst. A group of people escaped from an asylum and interbreeding to terrible genetic effect furthers the stigma of mental illness and muddies the issue of reproductive rights for people with intellectual disabilities. For us, this wasn't a tale we wanted to continue circulating.

The Frog People *(Bethel & Danbury):* Like the Melonheads, accounts of the so-called Frog People seem to indicate that they are (or were) human beings with significant birth defects. Digging deeper, though, revealed a sad tale about a possibly real family ridiculed, shunned from society, and living in abject poverty. Again, this wasn't a tale we felt comfortable perpetuating.

The Faceless People *(Monroe):* This is yet another legend that is often associated with the Melonheads and the Frog People. The story goes that a group of people with severe facial birth defects lives in a boarded up farmhouse somewhere in the woods of Monroe. The Faceless People are watched over by an elderly caretaker who escorts them out at night for fresh air. In addition to there being few reputable sources for this legend, it also raises the same problematic issues as the Melonheads and Frog People.

The Raggies *(Salisbury):* The Raggies are neither trolls nor subterranean mountain creatures, but a real group of people whose ancestors were possibly among the immigrant laborers who toiled at the Mt. Riga ironworks in Salisbury.

For more than 100 years between approximately the 1730s and 1840s, the forges on Mt. Riga contributed to the American Revolution, the War of 1812, and the general business of settling the wilds of North America. Many stories about the Raggies are couched in classist rhetoric and play into the fear of "the other" by portraying them as strange, dark, and short at best and impoverished, interbred, and unintelligent at worst. "In Connecticut, the Raggies are among those groups who have historically been subject to severe mistreatment," writes Stephen Gencarella in *Spooky Trails and Tall Tales: Connecticut*. As such, we felt it wouldn't be right to continue demonizing the Raggies by reprinting the stories told about them.

Other Connecticut Lore

Dudleytown *(Cornwall):* Strange animals or creatures are sometimes part of the Dudleytown legend, but Dudleytown seems to fall more squarely into the "haunted" category than the "cryptid" one. Besides, so much has already been written about Dudleytown — inaccuracies and otherwise — that it wasn't particularly exciting to revisit such well-trod ground. The Cornwall Historical Society has an excellent article titled "The Truth About Dudleytown" that cuts through a lot of the misinformation. As always, please note that Dudleytown is private property and that trespassers are often fined or arrested for going there.

The Moodus Noises *(East Haddam):* While the Moodus Noises are interesting phenomena that have birthed dozens of legends over hundreds of years, none surprisingly involve cryptids. Oh sure, the noises are thought to be caused by Native American deities or nature heroes, by Satan himself, by witches engaged in battle, and even by a giant precious stone — but not by cryptids!

Plum Island, the Montauk Monster & the Ocean Beach Creature *(New London):* While Plum Island and the Montauk Monster are interesting tales, neither is located in Connecticut. However, two months after the Montauk Monster appeared, a similar creature washed up at Ocean Beach in New London in September 2008. Are the two related? It's difficult to say since only one photo of the creature was taken and its body disappeared overnight.

The Yellow Mill Pond Serpent *(Bridgeport):* In Michael J. Bielawa's book *Wicked Bridgeport*, there's passing mention of a serpent that is rumored to live in Yellow Mill Pond. Michael and I had a very pleasant email exchange in which he explained that he had stumbled upon several tidbits and hints in newspaper microfilm archives about "something" in Yellow Mill Pond. Unfortunately, neither we nor the Bridgeport Community Historical Society could uncover any further reference to this beast.

The Ghost Dog of Town Hill *(Plymouth):* Judith Giguere's book *The Ghosts of Chippeny Hill* has a chapter about a ghost dog that appears to haunt Town Hill in Plymouth. However, this felt more like a ghost story, and even Giguere admits that there isn't much detail to the legend.

The Side Hill Goofus *(Glastonbury):* Several articles about the Glastonbury Glawackus mention a creature called the "Side Hill Goofus" as also residing in town. This seems to be another name for the Sidehill Gouger, Dodger, or Wampus, a cryptid that lives as far north as Vermont and as far south as North Carolina and Tennessee. The main characteristic of this beast is that it has evolved to living on hillsides, so the legs on one side of its body are shorter than those on the other. While there are stories about the Sidehill Gouger in other states, there doesn't seem to be any tales local to Connecticut, except those mentioning the Glawackus.

Essex Ed *(Essex):* A few folks pointed us to Essex Ed during our research, but this enormous groundhog statue is more of a town mascot than a cryptid. Since 1979, Essex Ed has presided over a boisterous parade each January from the Essex Boat Works on Ferry Street to the top of Main Street. Ed dresses in a new costume each year, selected to honor a special person or occasion. The costume is secret until the day of the parade. In addition, attendees are encouraged to bring their own noisemakers to the event, especially in the form of pots, pans, and tin cups.

"Red Eye" *(Franklin & various towns):* The book *Connecticut Lore* by Zachary Lamothe mentions an enigmatic entity known as "Red Eye" that supposedly lives in Ayers Gap in the town of Franklin. While details are scarce, this seems to be another story handed down via oral tradition among groups like the Boy Scouts. Other "red eye" stories exist throughout the state, usually with creatures seen in the dark that are indistinct except for sets of glowing red eyes. (See also the chapter on the Marsh Monster.)

Trappie *(Shelton):* A cryptid legend from the website *Damned Connecticut*, Trappie is a mysterious creature that haunts Trap Falls Reservoir in Shelton. By the site's own admission, they "tried to fabricate our own urban legend to no success."

Quassilla *(Middlebury):* Author Janis Hogan and illustrator Don Farrell produced a children's book about a plesiosaurus that lives in Lake Quassapaug. However, the character and story were invented solely for the book.

Famous horses *(Putnam, Bridgeport & Woodbury):* In addition to Carrie Welton's horse, Knight of the Forest (see page 93), several other horses of folklore are associated with Connecticut. The first is Rufus Malbone's beloved carthorse, Dolly. Rufus was a former enslaved person who was known for his incredible strength. To make a living, he bartered produce throughout the Putnam region after the Civil War. A common sight around town, Rufus and Dolly plied their trade until October 1884, when Rufus was injured in a wagon accident. Aware that death was near, Rufus asked that Dolly be buried with him. A marker for them exists near the Pomfret-Putnam town line to this day.

Another legend has to do with George Washington's visit to the Pixlee Tavern in Bridgeport. Washington was said to have arrived at the popular eatery on a particularly busy night in 1775 while on his way to Cambridge. Unable to find a table in which to enjoy the tavern's famous oysters, Washington told the astonished crowd how much his horse loved eating shellfish. The tavern patrons were clearly skeptical and piled a plate with oysters to try and entice Washington's horse. With the dining room now half-empty, Washington had no problem placing his dinner order. The tavern building still exists today, but as a private residence.

Finally, there's the story of Moll Cramer of Woodbury whose husband, Bill, bred racehorses. Moll was an incredible jockey who could earn the trust of nearly any animal, including horses. When her husband became jealous of her racing success, he barred her from competing. Nonetheless, she kept working at the stables until one day when a young colt threw an improperly fitted shoe during a race. Bill blamed his wife and beat her with a whip. She fled to Good Hill in Woodbury, and it wasn't long before Bill's fortunes took a turn. He blamed his wife for casting a spell on his horses and hung himself when he lost everything.

Moll lived the rest of her life in poverty on Good Hill. Those who were kind to her often received a bounty, like plentiful butter from the churn. But those who were stingy found themselves cursed with spoiled cream, rotten meat, or disease. Until her disappearance, Moll was known to be particularly kind to any horses, dogs, or children that stumbled upon her on Good Hill. Riders who let Moll pet their horses were rewarded with good foraging, and children usually returned with bucketsful of berries that were said to make extraordinary pies.

Real Creatures

Mountain lions *(various towns):* If you live in Connecticut long enough, you'll hear people talk about mountain lions. The CT Department of Energy and Environmental Protection (DEEP) claims that no breeding population of mountain lions lives in the state, yet the department receives 50-100 reports of supposed mountain lion sightings each year. According to an article in *Connecticut Magazine*, this has even led to conspiracy theories about a DEEP cover-up. Nonetheless, mountain lions (also known as cougars, pumas, catamounts, and panthers) are real creatures that do exist — just possibly not in Connecticut.

Black panthers *(Bristol & Canton):* Like mountain lions, stories of panthers occasionally pop up in Connecticut. With the exception of the "Killer Cat" of Granby, many of these stories amount to brief mentions without reliable sources or follow-up. For example, Val and I heard about a black panther that supposedly roamed the area between Rockwell Park and St. Joseph Cemetery in Bristol. Unfortunately, neither the Bristol Public Library nor the Bristol Historical Society were able to track down the source of this tale. Likewise, a brief unsigned article from the Nov. 30, 1950, issue of the *Hartford Courant* recounts how hunters in Canton encountered a "large cat-like black animal" that had allegedly killed several pigs in town. There is no word on whether the hunters ever caught their quarry.

Connecticut parrots *(various coastline towns):* The frigid coast of Connecticut is the last place one would expect to meet a colony of brightly colored South American parrots, but that's exactly where you'll find a large population of monk parakeets. No one is really sure how these birds got here, but they've been living in places like Stamford, Bridgeport, and Fairfield for the past 50 years. One theory is that the birds were born in captivity and released — accidentally or on purpose — only to adapt to Connecticut's climate. Monk parakeets live in large groups and build special nests that help keep them warm. So, yeah, a bunch of tropical birds really do live on the Connecticut coast.

Black squirrels and white squirrels *(various towns):* Many towns have sightings of squirrels that are completely black, while others have squirrels that are entirely white (but without the other traits of albinism, such as red eyes). Both are real varieties of the eastern gray squirrel, whose coat can be brown, gray, black, white, or russet.

The White Buffalo *(Goshen):* On June 16, 2012, a very special bison was born at Mohawk Bison farm in Goshen: one whose coat was entirely white. This calf didn't have albinism but was instead a 1 in 10 million genetic occurrence that is considered sacred by many Native American groups. For some, the white bison is a symbol of hope and unity; for others, it is a manifestation of the White Buffalo Calf Maiden prophet, or Ptesan Wi.

In the month after the calf's birth, hundreds of Native Americans visited Goshen to take part in a sacred naming ceremony for the calf. The white bison was officially dubbed Yellow Medicine Dancing Boy. As of this writing, he has lived safely at the farm his whole life and will never be sold or butchered for meat.

The Ledyard Lizard *(Ledyard):* Between July and August 2013, residents of Ledyard began seeing a giant lizard roaming around town. Photos of the reptile circulated online, with some mistakenly believing that it was an alligator. The

Ledyard Community Forum on Facebook even had t-shirts made to celebrate the "legend of the lizard." Unfortunately, the Ledyard Lizard was a very real creature that came to a very unfortunate end. On Aug. 25, 2013, the creature — which was, in fact, a four-foot-long Nile monitor lizard — raided a chicken coop before being shot by police. Its owner, from whom the creature had escaped, was charged with possession of an illegal reptile.

The Smith sisters and their cows *(Glastonbury):* Julia and Abby Smith were two elderly suffragists and abolitionists who refused to pay taxes to the town of Glastonbury in the 1870s because they were not allowed to vote. The town responded to their non-payment by seizing the sisters' pet Alderney cows and selling them at auction. One of the farmhands who worked at the property bought four of the cows and returned them to the sisters. The town later returned the other three.

However, this wasn't the last time that Glastonbury would confiscate the Smith cows in lieu of unpaid taxes. The cows were taken again twice in 1876, and each time the sisters bought them back after the cows had been sold at auction. By now, though, the story of cruel Glastonbury preying on two senior women had made national and even international headlines. Fearing for its public image, Glastonbury gave up trying to collect taxes from the Smith sisters.

ACKNOWLEDGEMENTS

Pat

While researching this book, I contacted countless historical
societies, museums, and libraries throughout Connecticut
and beyond, the vast majority of whom were incredibly
kind and gracious in offering assistance. Collecting these
stories would not have been possible without the people
who are devoted to preserving local history, most of whom
are volunteers. In particular, I'd like to recognize my
home library, the Howard Whittemore Memorial Library
in Naugatuck, which fielded most of my requests for
interlibrary loans.

In addition to local institutions, several people truly
went above and beyond to help see this project through
to completion. In no particular order, I'd like to offer my
sincerest thanks to:

Robert Adamczyk	Jenny Groome	Arthur Wiknik Jr.
David Leff	David Campbell	Barb Lessard
Diane Calabro	Ed Surato	Kurt Jovan
Meghan Glasgow	Carol Cheney	Meredith Bottino
Linda McKee	Ron Gagliardi	Zachary Lamothe
Meagan Cairns	Stephen Gencarella	Genevieve Coyle
Michael J. Bielawa	Shirley Sutton	Ramona Garcia
Judith Giguere	Christopher Shields	

I'd like to thank my good friend and collaborator, Val,
for going along with this crazy plan to write and illustrate
a book about Connecticut cryptids. Thank you to my
proofreaders Dee Kain Ruby Omen and Nick Vendetti for
reviewing the manuscript. Thank you also to Mathew Duman
for his publishing advice and design expertise in bringing
the book to life.

I owe a special debt of gratitude to members of the local
"Art Nite" group that was originally assembled by Val and
Dee. They frequently listened to stories as I found them and

were bombarded with "New Cryptid Alert!" messages in our group chat. I don't want to name them individually for fear of leaving someone out, but know that you all have my love and appreciation for critiquing various chapters of this book, even if I did choose to omit "Smooth Ned."

Finally, I'd like to thank my partner, Crystal, for her unending patience in listening to me prattle on about historical nonsense during the writing of this book, especially whenever I discovered something particularly interesting that I had to share *right. this. minute!*

While I have tried to diligently document my research in appropriate sources, any errors in facts or interpretation are strictly my own.

Val

First, I would like to thank my biggest supporter, the person who has been my rock in so many important ways, my partner, Dee (who was tied with Finn for the dedication ... but Finn won because we shared a womb. Sorry, beb!). It is so cliché to say, but I truly could not have finished this project without their encouragement. There were some days when I was compelled to keep going solely because of the misty, incredulous look in their eyes when I showed them the latest illustration. Thank you for believing in me when it was nearly impossible to do so on my own.

That leads me to my co-creator and author, Pat, a dear friend and truly the best possible creative partner for such an ambitious project. We are an unlikely duo, but somehow it just makes sense — and I think it makes what we've created together that much more meaningful. Thank you for holding me accountable just by virtue of you being such an immaculate professional. You're so good at this, and I'm truly honored to work with you. See ya in the next book!

I also want to thank my fellow members of the queer community in Connecticut. Early on in promoting this book at local vendor shows, my handmade sign that read, "ASK ME ABOUT CRYPTIDS!" lured so many curious queers to my table, like Mothman drawn to a floodlight. This has made me wonder if there are actually some cryptids hiding among us (Pat, take note!). The queer community's enthusiasm and willingness to adopt this project — and really, to adopt cryptozoology — reminds me of what I've always known: that queer is kind, and that we will always welcome the outcasts hiding on the outskirts of town or deep in the dark and endless woods.

Lastly, thank you to my parents, Nancy and Rick, and our little old Chihuahua-mix, Dewey (who may have a cameo somewhere in this book ... can you figure out where?). Thank you for always encouraging me to pursue art when other parents were encouraging jobs in offices. You've helped me grow into the cryptid-loving feral queer that I am today.

SOURCES

Southwestern Connecticut

The Candlewood Lake Monster

Murphy, Susan and Gary Smolen. *Images of America: Candlewood Lake.* Arcadia Publishing, 2005.

Ofgang, Erik. "Is There Really a Town Called Jerusalem and a Graveyard Under Candlewood Lake?"*Connecticut Magazine,* July 2019, www.ctinsider.com/ connecticutmagazine/news-people/article/Is-There-Really-a-Town-Called-Jerusalem-and-a-17044692.php. Accessed 9 Sept. 2021

Schoonover, Kristi Peterson. "Seven Creepy Tales of Candlewood Lake." *New England Horror Writers*, Aug. 13, 2016, nehw.blogspot.com/2016/08/legends-of-candlewood-lake-guest-blog.html. Accessed 9 Sept. 2021.

Sterry, Iveagh Hunt and William H. Garrigus. "Beneath Candlewood … The Big Basin." *They Found A Way.* Stephen Daye Press, Vermont, 1938: pp. 144-159.

"What Boaters Need to Know." *Candlewood Lake Authority,* candlewoodlakeauthority.org/What-Boaters-Need-to-Know. Accessed 12 Aug. 2022.

The Grench

"Dry Statistics Turn You Off? 'Grench' Help." *Greenwich Time*, March 21, 1975: pp. 3.

"Estimate Board Renames Editor." *Greenwich Time,* July 30, 1975: pp. 6.

"Meet the Grench." *Greenwich Time*, March 31, 1975: pp. 6.

Yudain, Carole Gewirtz. *The Greenwich Grench: Summary of the Annual Report for the Fiscal Year July 1973 to June 1974.* Illustrated by Mort Walker. Published by the Greenwich Board of Estimate and Taxation, February 1975.

Yudain, Carole Gewirtz. Personal interview. 28 Jan. 2022.

Sea Serpents

"Alarmed by Sea Serpent." *The Norwalk Hour*, June 29, 1904: pp. 5.

"Killed a 'Sea Serpent'." *The Norwalk Hour*, Sept. 30, 1902: pp. 1.

"Monster Sea Serpent." *The Evening Hour*, July 20, 1896: pp. 1.

News brief about sea serpent at Compo Beach. *The Norwalk Hour*, June 7, 1901: pp. 3.

News brief about sea serpent at Stratford Light. *The Norwalk Hour*, July 28, 1945: pp. 7

News brief about sea serpent with camel face. *The Norwalk Hour*, Jan. 15, 1934: pp. 4.

"Saw A Sea Serpent." *The Hartford Daily Courant*, Aug. 10, 1897: pp. 6.

"'Sea Serpent' at Play off Woodmont Shore." *The Norwalk Hour*, Aug. 1, 1913: pp. 1, 3.

"Sea Serpent at Roton." *The Norwalk Hour and The Westport Advertiser*, July 30, 1892: pp. 2.

"Sea Serpent in the Sound." *The Evening Hour*, Aug. 11, 1897: pp. 1.

"That Sea Serpent in the Sound." *The New York Times*, Sept. 5, 1878: pp. 5.

Perry Boney

"Chromolithograph entitled 'Custer's Last Fight'." *National Museum of American History Behring Center*, americanhistory.si.edu/collections/search/object/ nmah_326129. Accessed 10 Aug. 2022.

Muise, Peter. "Perry Boney, the Man Who Might Have Been A Fairy." *New England Folklore*, Feb. 28, 2016, newenglandfolklore.blogspot.com/2016/02/perry- boney-man-who-might-have-been.html. Accessed 10 Aug. 2022.

Murphy, Susan and Gary Smolen. *Images of America: Candlewood Lake*. Arcadia Publishing, 2005.

Ofgang, Erik. "Is There Really a Town Called Jerusalem and a Graveyard Under Candlewood Lake?" *Connecticut Magazine*, July 2019, www. ctinsider.com/connecticutmagazine/news-people/ article/Is-There-Really-a-Town-Called-Jerusalem- and-a-17044692.php. Accessed 10 Aug. 2022

Philips, David E. "Perry Boney." *Legendary Connecticut.* Curbstone Press, 1992. Originally published by Spoonwood Press, Hartford, 1984: pp. 39-42.

Sterry, Iveagh Hunt and William H. Garrigus. "Beneath Candlewood... The Big Basin." *They Found A Way.* Stephen Daye Press, Vermont, 1938: pp. 144-159.

The Lordship Mermaids

"A Brave Girl." *Evening Gazette*, July 12, 1897: pp. 1.

"Captain T. D. Judson Dead in Bridgeport." *The New York Times*, May 14, 1935: pp. 21.

D'Entremont, Jeremy. "The Kaptain's Kolumn #7." *U.S. Lighthouse Society News*, Aug. 7, 2018, news.uslhs. org/2018/08/07/the-kaptains-kolumn-7. Accessed 29 Aug. 2022.

"Donovan Effects Postponement of Judson Removal." *Bridgeport Evening Farmer*, Feb. 21, 1914: pp. 1.

"Donovan Inquires into Order Against Captain Judson." *Bridgeport Evening Farmer*, Feb. 20, 1914: pp. 1.

Fry, Ethan. "Deal with Coast Guard to open Stratford
    lighthouse to public." *CT Post*, June 10, 2019, www.
    ctpost.com/local/article/Stratford-inks-licensing-
    agreement-with-Coast-13965721.php. Accessed 29
    Aug. 2022.

"In Seven Days' Duel." *New-York Tribune*, Aug. 11, 1905:
    pp. 1.

"Judson and the Mermaid." *The Norwalk Hour*, Aug. 19, 1904:
    pp. 4.

News brief about Champlain Serpent. *Green Mountain
    Freeman*, Aug. 27, 1873: pp. 3.

Knapp, Lewis G. "Keepers of the Light." *Stratford and the Sea*.
    Arcadia Publishing, 2002: pp. 143-50.

Kunhardt Jr. Philip B., et al. "Selling the Public a Bogus
    Mermaid." *P.T. Barnum: America's Greatest Showman*.
    Alfred A. Knopf, 1995: pp. 40-43.

The Northwest Hills

The 'Killer Cat'

Allen, Francis. "Wild Animal Is Cat, Claims Dog Warden."
    Hartford Courant, June 25, 1959: pp. 10C.

---. "Claw Slaying Of Granby Cow Spurs Hunt For Phantom
    Killer." *Hartford Courant*, June 30, 1959: pp. 1A.

---. "Man Out For Lost Dog Spots Slinking Cat." *Hartford
    Courant*, July 8, 1959: pp. 6.

---. "Prints Prove Phantom A Cat, Says Zoologist." *Hartford Courant*, July 28, 1959: pp. 1.

Barrett, John. "'Killer Cat' Spotted In Simsbury; Described As Lean And Coal Black." *Hartford Courant*, July 6, 1959: pp. 1, 2.

---. "Dogs Killed Animals, Says Granby Officer." *Hartford Courant*, July 7, 1959: pp. 10A.

Bragdon, John. "5 Shots Miss 'Panther' At Barkhamsted Farm." *Hartford Courant*, July 18, 1959: pp. 1, 4.

---. "'Killer Cat' May Surprise Scoffers; Veterinarian Finds 4-Inch Paw Print." *Hartford Courant*, July 19, 1959: pp. 1A, 2A.

---. "'Panther' Fingerprinted At Barkhamsted Farm." *Hartford Courant*, July 20, 1959: pp. 4.

"Fontessa, Banker Says Big Barkhamsted Cat." *Hartford Courant*, May 11, 1960: pp. 27D.

"Game Officials Check Stories On Panther." *Hartford Courant*, June 23, 1959: pp. 10B.

"Granby 'Cat' Leaves Mark." *Hartford Courant*, March 23, 1960: pp. 16.

"Granby Terror No Panther But An Injun Devil." *Hartford Courant*, June 23, 1959: pp. 1A.

Messier Jr., Leon F. "'Panther' Paw Print Made By Dog, Says Zoologist." *Hartford Courant*, July 23, 1959: pp. 2.

"Safari In Darkest Granby Bags Nothing But Bugs." *Hartford Courant*, July 2, 1959: pp. 1.

"Safari Will Hit Trail Today To Hunt Elusive 'Killer Cat'." *Hartford Courant*, July 1, 1959: pp. 1.

"Track Of The Cat." *Hartford Courant*, May 11, 1960: pp. 26E.

"'Wanted Dead: Panther'." *Hartford Courant*, July 1, 1959: pp. 8.

"West Granby 'Panther' Seen By Truck Driver." *Hartford Courant*, June 21, 1959: pp. 2A.

"Wild Animal Report Sets Off Granby Area Search." *Hartford Courant*, Dec. 27, 1957: pp. 7.

"Will Eat Panther If Captured." *Hartford Courant*, July 10, 1959: pp. 5.

The Winsted Wildman

Bendici, Ray. "The CT Files: The Legend of the Winsted Wildman." *Connecticut Magazine*, Feb. 10, 2015, www.ctinsider.com/connecticutmagazine/news-people/article/The-CT-Files-The-Legend-of-the-Winsted-Wildman-17041808.php. Accessed 4 May 2022.

Citro, Joseph A. "Wild and Wily Wanderers." *Passing Strange: True Tales of New England Hauntings and Horrors*. David Diaz, illustrator. Houghton Mifflin, 1997: pp. 180-82.

Grigg, Bob. "The Winsted Wildman." *Historic Bytes*, The Colebrook Historical Society, www. colebrookhistoricalsociety.org/PDF%20Images/ The%20Winsted%20Wildman.pdf. Accessed 4 May 2022.

Harrell, Amy, et al. "Connecticut's Own Bigfoot: The Winsted Wild Man." *Fake News: Disinformation, Deception, and Magical Thinking Over Time*, Digital Scholarship Project, Trinity College, dsp.domains.trincoll.edu/ fake-news/fake-news/wildman. Accessed 4 May 2022.

"'Lou' Stone's Tallest Tales." *Hartford Courant*, Mar. 19, 1933: pp. D5.

O'Brien, Joseph A. "The 'Wild Man' May Be Back Again." *Hartford Courant*, Jul. 28, 1972: pp. 20C.

---. "Strange Creature Frightens Couples." *Hartford Courant*, Sept. 28, 1974: pp. 29C.

Philips, David E. "The Winsted Wild Man." *Legendary Connecticut*. Curbstone Press, 1992. Originally published by Spoonwood Press, Hartford, 1984: pp. 175-77.

"Smith, Riley W." *Winsted Directory, 1896-'97*. The Price & Lee Co., 1896: pp. 73.

"Town Officers of Winchester." *Winsted Directory, 1894-'95*. The Price & Lee Co., 1894: 106.

Wentworth, Frank L. *The Winsted Wildman and Other Tales*. Mercer Printing Company, Iowa City, Iowa, 1929: pp. 1-18.

"Wild Man Resumes Business." *The Evening Times*, Nov. 7, 1898: pp. 6.

The Old Men of the Mountains

Citro, Joseph A. "Wee New Englanders." *Passing Strange: True Tales of New England Hauntings and Horrors*. David Diaz, illustrator. Houghton Mifflin, 1997: pp. 143-147.

Hogan, Neil. "The Little People Inhabited the Berkshire." *New Haven Register*, Feb. 25, 1990.

Irving, Washington. "Rip Van Winkle." *Rip Van Winkle and Other Stories*. Susanne Suba, illustrator. Doubleday Junior Deluxe Editions, New York, 1955: pp. 7-33.

Lamothe, Zachary. "Old Men of the Mountains." *Connecticut Lore*. Schiffer, 2013: pp. 142.

The Giant Bat of Mine Hill

Bell, Michael and Diane B. Mayerfeld. *Time and the Land: The Story of Mine Hill*. Roxbury Land Trust and Yale School of Forestry and Environmental Studies, 1982.

Jovan, Kurt. Personal interview. 13 July 2021.

"Mine Hill: A 19th Century Iron-Making Complex." *Roxbury Land Trust*, www.roxburylandtrust.org/preserves mine-hill. Accessed 22 May 2022.

Whiteman, Lily. "The Night Life: Why We Need Bats All the Time — Not Just on Halloween." *National Science Foundation*, Oct. 31, 2012, www.nsf.gov/discoveries/ disc_summ.jsp?cntn_id=125883. Accessed 22 May 2022.

The Naugatuck Valley

The Goatman of the Opera House

Blitz, Matt. "The Goatman — Or His Story, at Least — Still Haunts Prince George's County." *Washingtonian*, Oct. 30, 2015, www.washingtonian.com/2015/10/30/the-goatman-or-his-story-at-least-still-haunts-prince-georges-county. Accessed 31 Oct. 2021.

Campbell, Joseph. *The Hero with a Thousand Faces.* Barnes & Noble Books (MJF Books), New York, 1997: pp. 81.

DaRosa, Andrew. "Ghost hunters claim to have spotted 'shadow people,' 'goat-humanoid' at Ansonia opera house." *New Haven Register*, May 11, 2021, www.nhregister.com/entertainment/article/Ghost-hunters-shadow-humanoid-Derby-opera-16168590.php. Accessed 24 Nov. 2021.

Gerry, Jeffrey. Personal interview. 23 Nov. 2021.

Hamilton, Edith. *Mythology: Timeless Tales of Gods and Heroes.* Warner Books, 1999: pp. 41-43.

Marrs, Jim. "Fishy Man-Goat Terrifies Couples Parked at Lake Worth." *Fort Worth Star-Telegram*, July 10, 1969: pp. 1.

O'Keefe, Marian. Personal interview. 3 Dec. 2021.

Vaughn, Chris. "Mystery Still Engulfs Lake Worth Monster." *NBC 5 Dallas-Fort Worth*, Aug. 6, 2009, www.nbcdfw.com/news/local/mystery-still-engulfs-lake-worth-monster/1879934. Accessed 31 Oct. 2022.

The High Rock Serpent

Beacon Falls Centennial 1871-1971. Published 1971.

Gencarella, Stephen. "Tragic Falls." *Spooky Trails and Tall Tales: Connecticut.* Falcon, 2019: pp. 122-127.

Orcutt, Samuel. *The Indians of the Housatonic and Naugatuck Valleys.* Press of the Case, Lockwood & Brainard Company, Hartford, 1882: pp. 40-48.

Skinner, Charles M. "Love and Rum." *Myths and Legends of Our Own Land: Vol. II.* J.P. Lippincott Company, Philadelphia, 1896: pp. 57-58.

The White Wolf of Peacedale Cemetery

"Arctic Wolf." *World Wildlife Fund,* www.worldwildlife.org/ species/arctic-wolf. Accessed 22 Sept. 2021.

Coleman, J.A. "wolf." *The Dictionary of Mythology.* Arcturus, 2007: pp. 1104.

"Coyote." *Connecticut Department of Energy and Environmental Protection,* portal.ct.gov/DEEP/ Wildlife/Fact-Sheets/Coyote. Accessed 22 Sept. 2021.

Ermenc, Christine. "Connecticut's Oldest Surviving Gravestone." *Windsor Historical Society,* July 31, 2017, windsorhistoricalsociety.org/connecticuts-oldest-surviving-gravestone. Accessed 27 Sept. 2022.

Giguere, Judith M. "The White Wolf of Peacedale." *The Ghosts of Chippeny Hill.* America Through Time, 2018: pp. 14-16.

The Marsh Monster

"Bristol." *Connecticut History, A CTHumanities Project*, connecticuthistory.org/towns-page/bristol. Accessed 28 Sept. 2022.

Giguere, Judith M. "The Monster of the Marsh." *The Ghosts of Chippeny Hill*. America Through Time, 2018: pp. 16-17.

Pitt, Steve. "Windigo." *The Canadian Encyclopedia*, March 8, 2018, www.thecanadianencyclopedia.ca/en/article/windigo. Accessed 23 Sept. 2021.

The Elves of Cheshire Village

Barbuto, Joan. "Family, 'Friendly Ghost' Share Home." *Nutmegger North*, Nov. 29, 1977: pp. 20-21

Cornell, Edith. "House At 125 Main Has Long History." *The Cheshire Herald*, Aug. 21, 1969. pp. 1, 4.

Gagliardi, Ron. *Images of America: Cheshire*. Arcadia Publishing, 2001: pp.12

The Little People Village

Bendici, Ray. "Little People's Village, Middlebury." *Damned Connecticut,* www.damnedct.com/little-peoples-village-middlebury. Accessed 10 April 2022.

Citro, Joseph A. "Little People Village." *Weird New England*. Sterling Publishing, 2005: pp. 268.

Ofgang, Erik. "The truth behind a mysterious 'fairy' village in the woods along I-84." *Connecticut Magazine*, Feb. 18, 2022, www.connecticutmag.com/the-connecticut-story/the-truth-behind-a-mysterious-fairy-village-in-the-woods-along-i-84/article_3080cbcc-4f4e-11ea-90d1-131166798d6b.html. Accessed 10 April 2022.

Rafford, Dr. Robert L. "Little People's Village mystery solved." *Bee-Intelligencer*, October 2015, Vol. XI, No. 11: pp. 5.

The Nauga

"A Legacy of Innovation." *Naugahyde*, www.naugahyde.com/about/history.cfm. Accessed 21 April 2022.

Leuchars, William G. "Charles Goodyear — Inventor." *Naugatuck Stories and Legends Volumes I & II*. Essex Printing, 2001. Originally published by Naugatuck Historical Society, 1969: pp. 58-62.

Mikkelson, David. "Naugahyde and the Nauga." *Snopes*, May 13, 2011, www.snopes.com/fact-check/naugahyde-and-seek. Accessed 21 April 2022.

"The Nauga® Shop." *Naugahyde,* www.naugahyde.com/dolls. Accessed 21 April 2022.

"A Nauga Story." *Naugahyde* via *Wayback Machine*, web.archive.org/web/20071217070050/http://www.naugahyde.com/history.html. Accessed 17 April 2022.

Buddy the Beefalo

Fox, Sandra Diamond. "'I almost got killed': CT farmer recounts corralling 'Buddy the beefalo'." *Connecticut Post*, April 15, 2021, www.ctpost.com/news/article/ There-are-many-heroes-in-this-story-Buddy-16103803. php. Accessed 13 July 2022.

Krasselt, Kaitlyn. "How to catch a beefalo: the true story of a police captain and his Bovine Bigfoot." *Connecticut Post*, Sept. 13, 2020, www.ctpost.com/middletown/ article/How-To-Catch-A-Beefalo-The-true-story- of-a-15563092.php. Accessed 13 July 2022.

"No second escape attempt for Buddy the beefalo at Critter Creek." *Tampa Bay Times*, June 20, 2021, www. tampabay.com/life-culture/pets/2021/06/20/no- second-escape-attempt-for-buddy-the-beefalo-at- critter-creek. Accessed 13 July 2022.

O'Neill, Tara. "Buddy the beefalo continues to elude Plymouth police." *Connecticut Post*, Dec.15, 2020, www.ctpost.com/news/article/Buddy-the-beefalo- continues-to-elude-Plymouth-15802061.php. Accessed 13 July 2022.

---. "'Buddy the beefalo' twice tries to escape pens at Florida sanctuary after 8 months on run in CT." *Connecticut Post*, April 23, 2021, www.ctpost.com/news/article/ Buddy-the-beefalo-twice-tries-to-escape-16124327. php. Accessed 13 July 2022.

---. "CT police raising money to buy Buddy the beefalo who escaped slaughterhouse." *Connecticut Post*, Sept. 7, 2020, www.ctpost.com/local/article/CT-police-raising-money-to-buy-Buddy-the-beefalo-15547640.php. Accessed 13 July 2022.

---. "Why Plymouth PD won't tranquilize Buddy the beefalo." *Connecticut Post*, Oct. 19, 2020, www.ctpost.com/policereports/article/Why-Plymouth-PD-won-t-tranquilize-Buddy-the-15658848.php. Accessed 13 July 2022.

Shay, Jim. "After 7 weeks on the lam, the latest on 'Buddy the Beefalo'." *Connecticut Post*, Sept. 22, 2020, www.ctpost.com/news/article/After-7-weeks-on-the-lam-the-latest-on-Buddy-15587513.php. Accessed 13 July 2022.

---. "Beefalo eludes capture 2 months after slaughterhouse escape." *Connecticut Post*, Oct. 6, 2020, www.ctpost.com/news/article/Beefalo-eludes-capture-2-months-after-15624300.php. Accessed 13 July 2022.

---. "'Buddy the Beefalo' — a 1,000-pound bull — remains free in CT woods." *Connecticut Post*, Sept. 3, 2020, www.ctpost.com/news/article/Buddy-the-Beefalo-a-1-000-pound-bull-15541000.php. Accessed 13 July 2022.

---. 'Buddy the Beefalo' makes rare appearance at Plymouth police trick-or-treat event." *Connecticut Post*, Oct. 24, 2020, www.ctpost.com/news/article/Buddy-the-Beefalo-makes-rare-appearance-at-15672516.php. Accessed 13 July 2022.

---. "Police: 'Highly aggressive' beefalo on the loose in CT." *Connecticut Post*, Aug. 28, 2020, www.ctpost.com/news/article/Police-Highly-aggressive-beefalo-on-the-15522596.php. Accessed 13 July 2022.

Yankowski, Peter. "Donors reach goal to rescue escaped CT beefalo, still on the run." *Connecticut Post*, Sept. 8, 2020, www. ctpost.com/local/article/Donors-reach-goal-to-rescue-escaped-CT-beefalo-15551494.php. Accessed 13 July 2022.

---. "Plymouth police: 'Buddy' the escaped beefalo will retire to Florida." *Connecticut Post*, Sept. 9, 2020, www. ctpost.com/local/article/Plymouth-police-Buddy-the-escaped-beefalo-15555377.php. Accessed 13 July 2022.

---. "Where's the beefalo? Buddy captured in Plymouth after more than 8 months." *Connecticut Post*, April 14, 2021, www.ctpost.com/news/article/Buddy-the-Beefalo-captured-in-Plymouth-16101594.php. Accessed 13 July 2022.

Carrie Welton's Horse, Knight

"Carrie Welton." *Colorado Encyclopedia*, coloradoencyclopedia.org/article/carrie-welton. Accessed 21 July 2022.

"Carrie Welton: A Rebel Before Her Time." *Mattatuck Museum*, www.mattmuseum.org/carrie-welton. Accessed 21 July 2022.

"Carrie Welton's Money: A Part of it Goes to a Hartford Sculptor." *Hartford Courant*, Sept. 19, 1887: pp. 8.

Guest, Raechel. "Welton Horse Fountain." *Waterbury Thoughts*, Nov. 26, 2016, waterburythoughts.blogspot.com/2016/11/welton-horse-fountain.html. Accessed 21 July 2022.

"Last Phase of the Welton Litigation." *Hartford Courant*, Dec. 31, 1884: pp. 3.

"More About Miss Welton's Will." *Hartford Courant*, Dec. 17, 1884: pp.3.

Pickering, James H. "'Alone Amid the Wind's Mad Revelry': The Death of Carrie Welton." *Colorado Heritage*, Summer 1998: pp. 2-13.

South Central Connecticut

The Downs Road Monster

Bache, R. Meade. "The Mad Mare of Mount Carmel, Connecticut. A Modern Myth." *Oliver Optic's Magazine*, Vol. 18, No. 265. Lee and Shepard, Boston, Aug. 1875: pp. 622.

Bailey, Hugh. "Woodbridge history book will feature houses, story of notorious ax murders." *New Haven Register*, Sept. 29, 2014, www.nhregister.com/connecticut/article/ Woodbridge-history-book-will-feature-houses-11363681.php. Accessed 28 Oct. 2022.

"Bethany History Timeline." *The Bethany Historical Society, Bethany, CT*, bethanyhistory.com/bethany-history-timeline. Accessed 28 Oct. 2022.

Colleran, Jim. "The Legend of Mad Mare's Hill." *A Walk Across the Giant*, Oct. 31, 2010, www.hikethegiant.blogspot. com/2010/10/legend-of-mad-mares-hill.html. Accessed 2 Sept. 2021.

Schmidt, James M. "'Murdered by a Maniac.'" *Murder by Gaslight*, March 9, 2013, www.murderbygaslight .com/2013/03/murdered-by-maniac-guest-post-by-james.html. Accessed 2 Sept. 2021.

Schurman, Kathleen. "Sperry Cemetery: A Murder by a Madman Rocks Bethany and Woodbridge." *Bethwood Patch*, Oct. 26, 2011, patch.com/connecticut/ bethwood/cemetery-4. Accessed 28 Oct. 2022.

Slater, Jacquie. "Halloween Haunts: A walk along Downs Road." *News 8 WTNH*, Oct. 29, 2016, www.wtnh.com/ news/connecticut/new-haven/halloween-haunts-a-walk-along-downs-road. Accessed 28 Oct. 2022.

"Terrible Affair with a Maniac." *Hartford Daily Courant*, Jan. 3, 1856: pp. 2.

Witches' Familiars

Barber, John Warner. "East Haven." *Connecticut Historical Collections*, 2nd Edition. Durrie & Peck and J.W. Barber, New Haven, 1836: pp. 208.

Bendici, Ray. "The CT Files: Hannah Cranna, 'The Wicked Witch of Monroe'." *Connecticut Magazine*, Oct. 12, 2015, www.ctinsider.com/connecticutmagazine/ article/The-CT-Files-Hannah-Cranna-The-Wicked-Witch-of-17041731.php. Accessed 26 Oct. 2021.

Monk, Ginny. "CT Senate absolves those accused of witchcraft." *Connecticut Mirror*, May 25, 2023, www.ctmirror.org/2023/05/25/ct-senate-absolves-accused-witchcraft. Accessed 14 June 2023.

Norman-Eady, Sandra and Jennifer Bernier, co-authors. "Connecticut Witch Trials and Posthumous Pardons." *OLR Research Report*, December 18, 2006 (2006-R-0718), www.cga.ct.gov/2006/rpt/2006-R-0718.htm. Accessed 26 Oct. 2021.

Philips, David E. "Hannah Cranna, the Wicked Witch of Monroe." *Legendary Connecticut*. Curbstone Press, 1992. Originally published by Spoonwood Press, Hartford, 1984: pp. 229-231.

---. "Debby Griffen." *Legendary Connecticut*. Curbstone Press, 1992. Originally published by Spoonwood Press, Hartford, 1984: pp. 259-261.

Toy, Ellie. "The Witches of East Haven." 2005. From the collection of the East Haven Historical Society.

"Witches and Witchcraft: The First Person Executed in the Colonies." *Tapping the Scales of Justice – A Dose of Connecticut Legal History*, State of Connecticut Judicial Branch Law Library Services, www.jud.ct.gov/lawlib/History/witches.htm. Accessed 26 Oct. 2021.

The Fair Haven Sea Dragons

"Historian's Corner: The Quinnipiac Oystering Community." *West Haven Voice*, Feb. 19, 2020, www.westhavenvoice.com/historians-corner-134. Accessed 07 Oct. 2021.

Knox, Jim. "The Harbor Seal Returns." *Greenwich Sentinel*, Jan. 24, 2020, www.greenwichsentinel. com/2020/01/24/the-harbor-seal-returns. Accessed 12 Oct. 2021.

Naumec, David J. "Native American Oystering." *Connecticut Explored*, Summer 2017, Vol. 15, No. 3: pp. 20-21.

Program for 1978 Fair Haven Festival, June 10-11, 1978, Howard Printing & Litho, New Haven, Conn.

Stephenson, Saundra. "Fair Haven Community and the Grand Avenue Bridge." *Bridges: Human Links and Innovations*, Yale-New Haven Teachers Institute, 2001 Volume V, Unit 5 (01.05.05), Section 7, teachersinstitute.yale.edu/curriculum/ units/2001/5/01.05.05/7. Accessed 12 Oct. 2021.

Townshend, Doris B. *Fair Haven: A Journey Through Time*. The New Haven Colony Historical Society, 1976: pp. 1-12, 16-19, 30-40, 56-57, 67-71.

The Sleeping Giant and Tuxis Island

Ackerman, Peter, producer. *Chief Richard O'Bamsawin | Odziozo*. YouTube, uploaded by Center for Research on Vermont, June 26, 2019, youtu.be/IBp92T3WqQ4. Accessed 21 March 2022.

"The Legend of Sampson Rock." Sampson Rock, Madison, Connecticut.

Lucey, Erin. "A Small Rock In Lake Champlain Has Deep Roots In Abenaki Mythology." Vermont Public Radio, Dec. 10, 2014, www.vpr.org/vpr-news/2014-12-10/a-small-rock-in-lake-champlain-has-deep-roots-in-abenaki-mythology. Accessed 21 Mar. 2022.

Marchi, Jason J. *The Legend of Hobbomock the Sleeping Giant.* Jesse J. Bonelli, illustrator. Fahrenheit Books, New Haven, 2011.

Simpson, Jennifer. "Tuxis Island." *Madison Neighbors*, Aug. 2021: pp. 18.

Tuccitto, Michelle. "Small Island Still Home to Legend of Giant." *The Shore Line Times*, July 13, 1994: pp. 3M.

The Black Dog of the Hanging Hills

Gencarella, Stephen. "Legendary Canines." *Spooky Trails and Tall Tales: Connecticut.* Falcon, 2019: pp. 73-76.

Harland, John and T.T. Wilkinson. "Demon and Goblin Superstitions." *Lancashire Folk-Lore: Illustrative of the Superstitious Beliefs and Practices, Local Customs and Usages of the People of the County Palatine.* Frederick Warne and Co., London, 1867: pp. 91-92.

"Hubbard Park." *City of Meriden*, www.meridenct.gov/city-services/parks-and-recreation/hubbard-park. Accessed 11 Nov. 2022.

MacKillop, James. "dog, dogs." *Dictionary of Celtic Mythology.* Oxford University Press, 2000. pp. 144-145.

---. "gwyllgi." *Dictionary of Celtic Mythology.* Oxford University Press, 2000. pp. 263.

---. "moddey dhoo." *Dictionary of Celtic Mythology.* Oxford University Press, 2000. pp. 332.

Ofgang, Erik. "The legend of the Black Dog of the Hanging Hills has its roots in literary lore." *Connecticut Magazine*, Jan. 19, 2021, www.connecticutmag.com/the-connecticut-story/the-legend-of-the-black-dog-of-the-hanging-hills-has-its-roots-in-literary/article_76dae24c-56a5-11eb-a582-c71c835cb573.html. Accessed 6 April 2022.

Pynchon, W.H.C. "The Black Dog." *The Connecticut Quarterly Vol. IV*. Copyright 1898 by George C. Atwell, Hartford CT: pp. 153-161.

Capitol Region

The Talcott Mountain 'Robot'

Citro, Joseph A. "Roaming Roadside Robots" *Weird New England*. Sterling Publishing, 2005: pp. 60-61.

"Mystery Robot Seen Roaming Talcott Mountain." *Hartford Courant*, Sept. 5, 1967: pp. 2.

"Remembering Dr. Donald P. La Salle." *Talcott Mountain Science Center*, www.tmsc.org/remembering-don-la-salle. Accessed 3 Mar. 2022.

"Science Center Head is Amused by 'Robot'." *Hartford Courant*, Sept. 6, 1967: pp. 32C.

The French Paymaster's Spectral Steed

Carlton, Lawrence S. "The French Paymaster's Ghost." *Canton Remembers: Incidents in Local History*. The Canton Historical Society, 2005: pp. 27-28.

Irving, Washington. "The Legend of Sleepy Hollow."*Rip Van Winkle and Other Stories.* Susanne Suba, illustrator. Doubleday Junior Deluxe Editions, New York, 1955: pp. 34-78.

Leff, David K. "The Headless Horseman of Canton." *David K. Leff: Essayist, Poet, Lecturer,* Oct. 31, 2015. www.davidkleff.typepad.com/home/2015/10/the-headless-horseman-of-canton.html. Accessed 9 Sept. 2021.

Philips, David E. "The Headless Horseman of Canton." *Legendary Connecticut.* Curbstone Press, 1992. Originally published by Spoonwood Press, Hartford, 1984: pp. 262-263.

"Saratoga: Freeman's Farm / Bemis Heights." *American Battlefield Trust,* www.battlefields.org/learn/revolutionary-war/battles/saratoga. Accessed 16 Nov. 2022.

Zeller, Bob. "The Tipping Point." *American Battlefield Trust,* June 25, 2018, www.battlefields.org/learn/articles/how-france-helped-win-american-revolution. Accessed 16 Nov. 2022.

The Creature in the Dairy Barn

"History of Moser Farm Dairy, an Ellington Icon." *Ellington Farmers Market,* Nov. 5, 2014, www.ellingtonfarmersmarket.org/single-post/2014/11/05/history-of-moser-farm-dairy-an-ellington-icon. Accessed 18 Nov. 2022.

Levick, Diane. "Bigfoot Is His Hobby." *Hartford Courant,* Aug. 15, 1983: pp. D1, D8.

MacKillop, James. "brownie." *Dictionary of Celtic Mythology.* Oxford University Press, 2000. pp. 60-61.

---. "bwci, bwcïod (pl.), bwca." *Dictionary of Celtic Mythology.* Oxford University Press, 2000. pp. 65.

---. "gruagach, gruacach, grógach." *Dictionary of Celtic Mythology.* Oxford University Press, 2000: pp. 260.

Muise, Peter. "A Monster in the Barn!." *New England Folklore*, Aug. 20, 2010, www.newenglandfolklore.blogspot. com/2010/08/monster-in-barn.html. Accessed 1 Jan. 2022.

Tarpey, John P. "'Bigfoot' Leaves Impression on 2 Ellington Farm Hands." *Hartford Courant*, Nov. 26, 1982: pp. A1, A8.

The Glawackus

Gencarella, Stephen. "On the Trail of the Glawackus." *Spooky Trails and Tall Tales:* Connecticut. Falcon, 2019: pp. 64-72.

"Glastonbury Wildcat May Be Hunted Today." *Hartford Courant*, Jan. 14, 1939: pp. 1.

"Glastonbury's What-Is-It." *Hartford Courant*, Jan. 15, 1939: pp. A2.

"Glawackus, Lost Until He Saw Map, Gives Exclusive Interview, Wags' Tail." *Hartford Courant*, Jan. 24, 1939: pp. 1, 7.

"Glawackus Lure For Hundreds." *Hartford Courant*, Jan. 31, 1939: pp. 14.

"Glawackus Must Appear If Bill Is To Be Passed." *Hartford Courant*, Feb. 9, 1939: pp. 6.

"Glawackus Track Is Discovered in Woods in Andover." *Hartford Courant*, Feb. 24, 1939. pp. 1, 6.

"Guffaws of Glastonbury Glawackus Greet Gloomy Gang of Gunners." *Hartford Courant*, Jan. 18, 1939: pp. 9.

"Hunters Search Today For Glastonbury 'Lion.'" *Hartford Courant*, Jan. 17, 1939: pp. 7

Johnson, Karl and Sarah Johnson. "Caveboy Johnson Turns 90." *Digital Amherst*, www.digitalamherst.org/ exhibits/show/the-johnsons-of-hockanum/caveboy-johnson-turns-90. Originally published in the *Springfield Republican*, Feb. 2, 2018. Accessed 20 Jan. 2022.

"Mysterious Glawackus Is No More." *Hartford Courant*, July 7, 1939: pp. 1, 8.

"Safari Treks, 'Wild Beast' To Stalk, Gets One Fox and Eight-Mile Walk." *Hartford Courant*, Jan. 15, 1939: pp. 1, 12.

"'Scientist' Who Named Glawackus Was Courant Man." *Hartford Courant*, Jan. 25, 1939: pp. 1.

"Wanted! Dead or Alive the 'Glastonbury Glawackus'!" *Hartford Courant*, advertising section, Jan. 24, 1939: pp. 10.

The Pterodactyl

Adelman, Lorraine. "Pterodactyl Season Opens After 500 Million Years." *Hartford Courant*, Jan. 22, 1956: pp. 1, 4, 8.

"Glastonbury Schedules Pterodactyl Hunt Day." *Hartford Courant*, Jan. 18, 1956: pp. 20.

"A Little Mammoth Meat, Please, Sportsmen Ask." *Hartford Courant*, Jan. 9, 1957: pp. 1.

Murphy, Thomas E. "Of Many Things — Pterodactyls." *Hartford Courant*, Jan. 12, 1956. pp. 12.

Stevenson, E. Robert. "Yankee Editor Around the World: After Seeing Australia I Can Believe In Glastonbury's Pterodactyl." *Hartford Courant*, April 8, 1956: pp. 5B.

Lower Connecticut River Valley

The Shad Spirit

"American shad." *U.S. Fish & Wildlife Service Fish and Aquatic Conservation*, www.fws.gov/fisheries/freshwater-fish-of-america/american_shad.html. Accessed 16 Sept. 2021.

Brainard, John G.C. "The Shad Spirit." *The Poems of John G.C. Brainard: A New and Authentic Collection, with an Original Memoir of His Life*. Edward Hopkins, Hartford, 1842: pp. 21-23, 190.

Gencarella, Stephen. "Hunting the Connecticut River
    Oddities." *Spooky Trails and Tall Tales: Connecticut.*
    Falcon, 2019: pp. 53-54.

Hesselberg, Erik. "The Shad Spirit." *Estuary*, March 2, 2020,
    www.estuarymagazine.com/2020/03/the-shad-
    spirit-2. Accessed 16 Sept. 2021.

---. "The Spirit of the Shad." *The Middletown Press*, April 2,
    2002, www.middletownpress.com/news/article/The-
    spirit-of-the-shad-11928268.php. Accessed 16 Sept.
    2021.

The Black Fox of the Salmon River

Brainard, John G.C. "The Black Fox of the Salmon River." *The
    Poems of John G.C. Brainard: A New and Authentic
    Collection, with an Original Memoir of His Life.* Edward
    Hopkins, Hartford, 1842: pp. 82-84.

---. "Salmon River." *The Poems of John G.C. Brainard: A New
    and Authentic Collection, with an Original Memoir of
    His Life.* Edward Hopkins, Hartford, 1842: pp. 80-82.

Gencarella, Stephen. "Legendary Canines." *Spooky Trails and
    Tall Tales: Connecticut.* Falcon, 2019: pp. 76-78.

Muise, Peter. "The Black Fox." *New England Folklore*, Feb. 23,
    2009, www.newenglandfolklore.blogspot.com/2009/
    02/black-fox.html. Accessed 24 Sept. 2021.

Philips, David E. "The Black Fox of Salmon River." *Legendary
    Connecticut.* Curbstone Press, 1992. Originally
    published by Spoonwood Press, Hartford, 1984: pp.
    256-58.

Whittier, John Greenleaf. "The Black Fox." *Poems*. New York Publishing Company, 1895: pp. 83-88.

Williams, Roger. *A Key into the Language of America*. Howard M. Chapin, introduction. Applewood Books, 1997: pp.103.

The Connecticut River Serpent

"Again the Sea Serpent." *The Victorian Express*, June 16, 1888: pp. 3.

"Connecticut River: New England Strong." *American Rivers*. www.americanrivers.org/river/connecticut-river. Accessed 2 Dec. 2021.

"The Connecticut River Serpent." *Strange New England*, Oct. 9, 2017, www.strange-new-england.com/2017/10/09/the-connecticut-river-serpent. Accessed 3 Dec. 2021.

"CT River Watershed Facts." *Connecticut River Conservancy*. www.ctriver.org/learn/watershed-facts. Accessed 2 Dec. 2021.

Gencarella, Stephen. "Hunting the Connecticut River Oddities." *Spooky Trails and Tall Tales: Connecticut*. Falcon, 2019: pp. 48-52.

"The Park River." *Bushnell Park Foundation*. www.bushnellpark.org/about-2/history-2/the-park-river. Accessed 2 Dec. 2021.

"A River 'Sea Serpent'." *The Penn's Grove Record*, May 25, 1894: pp. 1.

"That Annoying Sea Serpent." *The New York Times*, Sept. 9, 1886: pp. 1.

Moshup the Giant

Bellincampi, Suzan. "Moshup's Toad." *Vineyard Gazette*, Dec. 10, 2020. vineyardgazette.com/news/2020/12/10/moshups-toad. Accessed 26 Dec. 2021.

Fawcett, Melissa Jayne. "Moshup's Rock." *The Lasting of the Mohegans: Part 1*. Pequot Printing, Ledyard, Conn., 1995: pp. 48-49.

Gencarella, Stephen. "The Devil's Hopyard." *Spooky Trails and Tall Tales: Connecticut*. Falcon, 2019: pp. 39-47.

"Moshup, the Giant." *Mohegan Tribe*. www.mohegan.nsn.us/explore/heritage/our-stories/moshup-the-giant. Accessed 26 Dec. 2021.

Tantaquidgeon Zobel, Melissa. "Mohegan Sacred Sites: Moshup's Rock." *ConnecticutHistory.org*, July 2, 2021, connecticuthistory.org/mohegan-sacred-sites-moshups-rock. Accessed 26 Dec. 2021.

Bigfoot's Visit to Connecticut

Bendici, Ray. "Bigfoot in Connecticut?" *Damned Connecticut*, www.damnedct.com/bigfoot-in-connecticut. Accessed 4 Oct. 2021.

"Bigfoot Loves a Barbecue." *Finding Bigfoot*, season 4, episode 5, Animal Planet, 13 March 2013. Amazon Prime Video, www.amazon.com/gp/video/detail/B00BECZQA2/ref=atv_dp_season_select_s4

"Cotton Hollow Wild Man." *Naugatuck Daily News*, June 29, 1898: pp. 4

"Report # 13585." *The Bigfoot Field Researchers Organization*, Jan, 16, 2006, www.bfro.net/GDB/show_report asp?id=13585. Accessed 4 Oct. 2021.

"Report # 69612." *The Bigfoot Field Researchers Organization*, Aug. 26, 2021, www.bfro.net/GDB/show_report. asp?id=69612. Accessed 4 Oct. 2021.

The Glowackus, Successor to the Glawackus

Bastian, Richard. "State Police Considering Arrests in Monster Hoax." *New Haven Register*, Sept. 17, 1966.

"Glowackus Creator Says He Sought Only Laughs." *The New Era*, Sept. 22, 1966: pp. 1, 7.

Knapp, Fred. "Horsemen Encounter Creature; Believed To Be 'Glowackus'." *The New Era*, Sept. 15, 1966: pp. 1, 6.

Stannard, Charles. "A Tall Tale of a Terrifying Beast in the Woods." *Hartford Courant*, Nov. 17, 2000, www. courant.com/news/connecticut/hc-xpm-2000-11-17-0011171087-story.html. Accessed 08 Jan. 2022.

The Higganum Mucket

Day, Cassandra. "Haddam's Mucket Madness Day to fete mystical creature with fearsome teeth." *Middletown Press*, March 27, 2020, www.middletownpress.com/news/article/Haddam-s-Mucket-Madness-Day-to-fete-mystical-15162904.php. Accessed 25 Feb. 2022.

"Historic Flood June 1982." *National Weather Service*, www. weather.gov/nerfc/hf_june_1982. Accessed 25 Feb. 2022.

Vincent, Wendy. "Higganum Muckets Invade Killingworth Library." *The Haddams-Killingworth Patch*, July 11, 2012, patch.com/connecticut/thehaddams-killingworth/higganum-muckets-invade-killingworth-library. Accessed 25 Feb. 2022.

Wiknik Jr., Arthur. "The Higganum Mucket." 2012. Courtesy of the author.

---. "Mucket Mania." *Heading Out,* Summer 1987: pp. 8-9.

---. "Mucket Mania II." *Heading Out*, Nov. 1989: pp. 8-11.

---. "Mucket Mania III: The Madness Continues." *Heading Out*, May 1990: pp. 16-18.

---. "The Mucket Recovery Program." 2009. Courtesy of the author.

The Old Saybrook Blockheads

"Alumni Records Office, Yale University, Records of Alumni from the Classes of 1701-1978 (RU 830)." Manuscripts and Archives, Yale University Library. archives.yale. edu/ repositories/12/archival_objects/957464. Accessed August 19, 2022.

Bradshaw, Betty. "'One-Woman USO' Makes Essex Bit of Old England for Sailors." *Hartford Courant*, Nov. 1, 1942: pp. 1.

"Connecticut Casualties." *Hartford Courant*, June 12, 1945: pp. 5.

"Mary M. Geran Starr Papers." Manuscripts and Archives, Yale University Library.archives.yale.edu/repositories/ 12/resources/2964. Accessed August 19, 2022.

Mebane, Lex. "The Near-Landing at Old Saybrook, Connecticut, December 16, 1957." *The Collected Issues of the CSI News Letter: Civilian Saucer Intelligence Group*. Saucerian Publisher, 2020: pp. 113-14.

"Mrs. Starr is Going Abroad with Pupils." *Hartford Courant*, May 27, 1947: pp. 2.

Revai, Cheri. "The Starr Encounter." *Haunted Connecticut*. Stackpole Books, 2006: pp. 57-58.

"Slander Suit Brought by Mrs. Starr." *Hartford Courant*, Nov. 23, 1945: pp. 11.

Starr, Mary M. "Europe's Newest King, Who Studies Tropical Diseases for Fun Sketched by Former E. Hartford Teacher, Friend of His Family." *Hartford Courant*, Oct. 27, 1935: pp. D3.

"Thanked by Parliament." *Hartford Courant*, April 4, 1943: pp. 3.

Northeastern Connecticut

The Battle of the Frogs

"American Bullfrog (Rana catesbeiana)." *Beardsley Zoo*, www. beardsleyzoo.org/american-bullfrog.html. Accessed 2 Aug. 2022.

"The Battle of the Frogs." *Windham Historical Society*, windhamhistoricalsociety.org/the-battle-of-the-frogs. Accessed 2 Aug. 2022.

"Great Awakening." *History.com*, March 7, 2018, www.history.com/topics/british-history/great-awakening. Accessed 2 Aug. 2022.

Hoberman, Michael. "Bridge Ornaments Help Tell the Legend of the Windham Frog Fight." *ConnecticutHistory.org*, June 8, 2021, connecticuthistory.org/bridge-ornaments-help-tell-the-legend-of-the-windham-frog-fight. Accessed 2 Aug. 2022.

Payne, Brigham. *The Story of Bacchus and Centennial Souvenir*. A.E. Brooks, Hartford, 1876.

Philips, David E. "The Windham Frog Fight." *Legendary Connecticut*. Curbstone Press, 1992. Originally published by Spoonwood Press, Hartford, 1984: pp. 215-218.

Wadsworth, Kimberly. "A Connecticut Town's Tribute to a Bullfrog Battle." *Atlas Obscura*, Feb. 3, 2014, www.atlasobscura.com/articles/a-connecticut-town-s-tribute-to-a-bullfrog-battle. Accessed 2 Aug. 2022.

The White Deer

Bestul, Scott. "I Passed Up an Albino Buck. And a Piebald Doe. The Reasons Why May Surprise You." *Field & Stream*, Jan. 11, 2022, www.fieldandstream.com/hunting/shooting-an-albino-deer. Accessed 3 Aug. 2022.

Miller, Matthew L. "White Deer: Understanding a Common Animal of Uncommon Color." *Cool Green Science*, Feb. 3, 2016, blog.nature.org/science/2016/02/03/white-deer-understanding-a-common-animal-of-uncommon-color. Accessed 3 Aug. 2022.

Zimmerman, Larry E. "The Rendering Pit." Courtesy of the Center for Woodstock History (Woodstock Historical Society, Inc.), 2004.018Ms036.

Southeastern Connecticut

The Worrineagues

Gencarella, Stephen. "An Accursed Spot." *Spooky Trails and Tall Tales: Connecticut.* Falcon, 2019: pp. 178-79.

Ladd, Eleanor Mary. "Old Franklin: Interesting Sketch of a Connecticut Town." *Hartford Courant*, Sept. 25, 1894: pp. 10.

Marshall, Bridget M. "Mary (Reeve) Webster, the 'Witch' of Hadley." From a talk given May 2003. faculty.uml.edu//bmarshall/Mary%20Webster.htm. Accessed 10 Jan. 2022.

S.W.A. "Wollaneags and Worraneags." *Hartford Courant*, Oct. 3, 1894: pp. 1.

The Horse Creature

Lamothe, Zachary. "Creatures of the Woodland." *Connecticut Lore.* Schiffer, 2013: pp. 70-71.

MacKillop, James. "cabyll-ushtey." *Dictionary of Celtic Mythology*. Oxford University Press, 2000. pp. 66.

---. "ceffyl dwfr, dŵr." *Dictionary of Celtic Mythology*. Oxford University Press, 2000. pp. 83.

---. "each uisce, each uisge, aughisky." *Dictionary of Celtic Mythology*. Oxford University Press, 2000. pp. 164.

---. "kelpie, kelpy, waterkelpie." *Dictionary of Celtic Mythology*. Oxford University Press, 2000. pp. 281.

Wheeler, Jim. Personal interview. 26 May 2022 – 07 July 2022.

The Jewett City Vampires

Bell, Michael E. "Never Strangers True Vampires Be." *Food for the Dead: On the Trail of New England's Vampires*. Carroll & Graf Publishers, New York, 2001: pp. 156-177.

Citro, Joseph A. "The Hungry Dead." *Passing Strange: True Tales of New England Hauntings and Horrors*. David Diaz, illustrator. Houghton Mifflin, 1997: pp. 204-19.

Nalewicki, Jennifer. "See the face of an 18th century 'vampire' buried in Connecticut." *Live Science*, Oct. 31, 2022, www.livescience.com/vampire-burial-dna-connecticut. Accessed 16 Jan. 2023.

Ofgang, Erik. "The mystery of a Connecticut 'vampire' has been solved." *Connecticut Magazine*, Sept. 19, 2019, www.connecticutmag.com/history/the-mystery-of-a-connecticut-vampire-has-been-solved/article_043e33c2-d4c6-11e9-80a6-1b717e11b783.html. Accessed 08 Feb. 2022.

Philips, David E. "The Jewett City Vampires." *Legendary Connecticut*. Curbstone Press, 1992. Originally published by Spoonwood Press, Hartford, 1984: pp. 245-46.

Tucker, Abigail. "The Great New England Vampire Panic." *Smithsonian Magazine*, October 2012, www.smithsonianmag.com/history/the-great-new-england-vampire-panic-36482878. Accessed 08 Feb. 2022.

The Pigman

Levitt, Alice. "Local Legends." *Seven Days*, Oct. 28, 2009, www.sevendaysvt.com/vermont/local-legends/Content?oid=2138659. Accessed 26 April 2022.

McInvale, Courtney. "Legends and Folklore of the Mystic River." *Haunted Mystic*. Haunted America, 2014: pp. 115-18.

The Makiawisug

Bendici, Ray. "The Makiawisug (The Little People) of Mohegan Hill, Uncasville." *Damned Connecticut*, www.damnedct.com/the-makiawisug-the-little-people-of-mohegan-hill-uncasville. Accessed 5 July 2022.

Citro, Joseph A. "Wee New Englanders." *Passing Strange: True Tales of New England Hauntings and Horrors.* David Diaz, illustrator. Houghton Mifflin, 1997: pp. 145.

"Eastern Whip-poor-will (Antrostomus vociferous)." *National Audubon Society*, www.audubon.org/field-guide/bird/ eastern-whip-poor-will. Accessed 11 July 2022.

Fawcett, Melissa Jayne. "Makiawisug Mounds." *The Lasting of the Mohegans: Part 1*. Pequot Printing, Ledyard, Conn., 1995: pp. 49-50, 58.

Fawcett, Melissa Jayne and Joseph Bruchac. *Makiawisug: The Gift of the Little People.* David Wagner, illustrator. Little People Publications, a licensee of the Mohegan Tribe, 1997.

Forrest, Daniel T. "The Villages — A Proposed 120-unit Apartment Community Complex, Montville, CT." Sept. 13, 2012, *State Historic Preservation Office*, www. theday.com/ assets/pdf/NL124841921.PDF. Accessed 5 July 2022.

"Gladys Tantaquidgeon." *Mohegan Tribe*, www.mohegan.nsn. us/explore/heritage/memoriam/medicine-woman- gladys-tantaquidgeon-memorial. Accessed 5 July 2022.

"Makiawisug, or the Little People." *Mohegan Tribe*, www. mohegan.nsn.us/explore/heritage/our-stories/ makiawisug. Accessed 5 July 2022.

"Mohegan Chiefs of the 20th Century." *Mohegan Tribe*, www. mohegan.nsn.us/about/our-tribal-history/ceremonial- leaders/chiefs-of-the-20th-century. Accessed 23 Jan. 2023.

Muise, Peter. "The Little People Who Live Under the Hill." *New England Folklore*, June 29, 2014, newenglandfolklore.blogspot.com/2014/06/the-little-people-who-live-under-hill.html. Accessed 5 July 2022.

Santiago, Ellyn. "Mohegan Tribe's Cultural Boundary Reduced But Still Could Block Affordable Housing." *Montville Patch*, Sept. 24, 2012, patch.com/connecticut/montville-ct/mohegan-tribe-s-cultural-boundary-reduced-but-still-cf43f7b1f78. Accessed 5 July 2022.

"Shantup, Martha, 1761 - 1859." *Native Northeast Portal*, nativenortheastportal.com/bio/bibliography/shantup-martha-1761-1859. Accessed 5 July 2022.

"Smith, Fidelia Ann Hoscott, 1827 - 1908." *Native Northeast Portal*, nativenortheastportal.com/bio/bibliography/smith-fidelia-ann-hoscott-1827-1908. Accessed 11 July 2022.

But What About ...?

Applebome, Peter. "A Bison So Rare It's Sacred." *The New York Times*, July 12, 2012, www.nytimes.com/2012/07/13/nyregion/sacred-white-bison-is-born-in-rural-connecticut.html. Accessed 24 Jan. 2022.

Bendici, Ray. "Sea Monsters & Serpents, Long Island Sound." *Damned Connecticut*, www.damnedct.com/sea-monsters-serpents-long-island-sound. Accessed 15 July 2022.

Bielawa, Michael J. *Wicked Bridgeport*. The History Press, 2012: pp. 103.

Boyle, Lindsay. "Ledyard Community Forum offers help, tips and friendship." *The Day*, July 14, 2015, www.theday.com/article/20150714/NWS01/150719614. Accessed 23 March 2022.

Brown, Charles E. "Sidehill Dodger." *Paul Bunyan Natural History*, C.E. Brown, Wisconsin, 1935: pp. 5.

Citro, Joseph A. "The Farm of the Faceless People." *Weird New England.* Sterling Publishing, 2005: pp. 65.

Gencarella, Stephen. "The Raggies." *Spooky Trails and Tall Tales*: Connecticut. Falcon, 2019: pp. 128-135.

Giguere, Judith M. "The Ghost Dog of Town Hill." *The Ghosts of Chippeny Hill.* America Through Time, 2018: pp. 35-36.

"Hundreds gather in Connecticut to celebrate the birth of a rare white bison." *MassLive*, July 29, 2012, www.masslive.com/news/2012/07/hundreds_gather_in_connecticut.html. Originally published by the Associated Press. Accessed 24 Jan. 2022.

"Hunters Wait For Winter To Bag Canton 'Panther'." *Hartford Courant*, Nov. 30 1950: pp. 1.

Lamothe, Zachary. "Creatures of the Woodland." *Connecticut Lore.* Schiffer, 2013: pp. 70-71.

McCain, Diana Ross. "Abby Smith and Her Cows." *It Happened in Connecticut.* Two Dot, an imprint of Globe Pequot, 2008: pp. 93-98.

Morga, Adriana. "Did you know there are wild monk parakeets in Connecticut?" *CT Insider*, July 30, 2021, www.ctinsider.com/living/article/Did-you-know-about-Connecticut-s-Monk-Parakeets-16352275.php. Accessed 08 April 2022.

"Mysterious Creature Spotted In New London." NBC 30, Sept. 29, 2008, via *Wayback Machine*, web.archive.org/web/20081002003250/http://www.nbc30.com/news/17584475/detail.html. Accessed 15 July 2022.

Ofgang, Erik. "There are no mountain lions in Connecticut, so why do we keep seeing them?" *Connecticut Magazine*, Oct. 24, 2019, www.ctinsider.com/connecticutmagazine/article/There-are-no-mountain-lions-in-Connecticut-so-17044867.php. Accessed 9 Sept. 2021

Owens, David. "Police Charge Ledyard Lizard Owner." *Hartford Courant*, Sept. 13, 2013: pp. B4.

Philips, David E. "George Washington's Horse." *Legendary Connecticut.* Curbstone Press, 1992. Originally published by Spoonwood Press, Hartford, 1984: pp. 106-108.

---. "Legends of Mr. Riga." *Legendary Connecticut.* Curbstone Press, 1992. Originally published by Spoonwood Press, Hartford, 1984: pp. 186-191.

---. "The Moodus Noises." *Legendary Connecticut.* Curbstone Press, 1992. Originally published by Spoonwood Press, Hartford, 1984: pp. 199-203.

---. "Rufus Malbone." *Legendary Connecticut.* Curbstone Press, 1992. Originally published by Spoonwood Press, Hartford, 1984: pp. 95-97.

Shay, Jim. "Rare white squirrel spotted in Westport." *Connecticut Post*, Jan. 15, 2016, www.ctpost.com/news/article/Rare-white-squirrel-spotted-in-Westport-6761061.php. Accessed 23 Sept. 2021.

Sterry, Iveagh Hunt and William H. Garrigus. "Moll Cramer ... The Witch of Woodbury." *They Found A Way*. Stephen Daye Press, Vermont, 1938: pp. 273-281.

"The Truth About Dudleytown." *Cornwall Historical Society*, Sept. 29, 2014, www.cornwallhistoricalsociety. blogspot.com/2014/09/the-truth-about-dudleytown. html. Accessed 22 Sept. 2021.

ABOUT THE RESEARCHERS

A native of Naugatuck, **Patrick Scalisi** achieved a certificate in Cryptid Field Observation Studies from Nutmeg State University. His primary focus is on composing written notes of cryptid behavior and appearance while examining these creatures in their native habitats. Aside from his cryptid research, Pat has been known to write about much more fanciful topics like fantasy worlds and outer space. His youth sci-fi novel, *The Key to the Universe*, is available from Owl Hollow Press.

In his spare time, Pat often sheds his guise of a responsible adult to play video games, build Lego models, and generally be a nerd. He lives in Naugatuck with his partner, Crystal, and their cadre of cats.

Valerie Ruby-Omen is a professional artist who earned a certificate in Cryptid Illustrative Works from Constitution State College. Her love for the glorious state parks and natural wonders of Connecticut led her deep into the woods, where she found her true calling as a cryptid field artist. With her work of cataloging every Connecticut cryptid now complete, she plans on taking a quick break to sample an iced latte from every coffee shop in the state.

When Valerie isn't creating art ... just kidding, she's always creating art. You can find her moonlighting on various projects at The Tiny Ruby Illustrations. She lives blissfully in Naugatuck with her partner, Dee, and their tiny black cat named Ashiok.

www.ingramcontent.com/pod-product-compliance
Lightning Source LLC
Chambersburg PA
CBHW071556150726

48000CB00004B/1486